The Spa Life *at home*

MARGARET PIERPONT *and* DIANE TEGMEYER

photography by Jill Uris

LONGSTREET PRESS, INC.

Atlanta, Georgia

For our parents
Edith and John Pierpont
Phyllis and Robert Tegmeyer

Published by

LONGSTREET PRESS, INC.

A subsidiary of Cox Newspapers,

A subsidiary of Cox Enterprises, Inc.

2140 Newmarket Parkway

Suite 122

Marietta, GA 30067

Printed in the United States of America

1st printing, 1997

Library of Congress Catalog Card Number: 96-79802

ISBN: 1-56352-372-8

Jacket and book design by Jill Dible

Contents

Acknowledgments

No book can ever be done without support from others. We have been lucky to have generous families, friends and colleagues who have offered encouragement every step of the way. We would like to express our deepest gratitude for the time and expertise given by many people in the spa world, to those who shared their ideas and to those too numerous to mention, who guided us through the spa experience. In particular, we would like to thank the following:

The Anara Spa at the Hyatt Regency Kauai: Meryl Pearlstein, Shelley Widen-Hall; Bonaventure Resort and Spa: Christine Felty, Tanya Lee, Christine Wherry; The Broadmoor: Rose Abello, Marguerite Lykes; Canyon Ranch: Katie Garber, Lana Holstein, Julie Waltz Kembel, John Luzader, Holly McCarter, Hanna Soule; The Claremont Resort and Spa: John Defonts, Henry Feldman, Ron Hechman, Nancy Minges, Linda Prout, Candace Taylor; The Cooper Aerobics Center: Kathleen Duran, Leah Kay Gabriel, T. L. Mitchell, M.D.; The Crescent Court: Steve Hancock, Deborah Kern, Wendy Walker; Doral Golf Resort and Spa: Kathleen Casper, Deborah Daley, Jossie Feria, Bruce Fox, Kathie Graham; Golden Door: Judy Bird, Richard Bird, Ann Harriet Buck, Rachel Caldwell, Mary Elizabeth Gifford, Marcia Kitson, Kathleen Martin, Michel Stroot; The Greenhouse: Leopoldo Gonzalez, Shirley Ogle, John Painter; Green Valley Spa and Tennis Resort: Alan Coombs, Carol Coombs, Gwen Moon, Jim Root; Ihilani Resort & Spa: Ann Emich, Christine Stanton; Lake Austin Spa Resort: Terry Conlan, Cindy Present, Lynne Vertrees; Miraval Life in Balance: Erika Dills, William Elliott, Bruce Martin, Cary Neff, Reed Smith, Steve Stone, David Tate; Norwich Inn and Spa: Betty Loicono, Debbie Peterson; The Peaks at Telluride: Gayle Moeller-Brady, Bonnie Ketering; PGA National Resort and Spa: Ann Bramham, Mary Gendron, Cheryl Hartsough, Sherrie Luis, Caryn Shoffner; Rancho La Puerta: Barbara Abrahams, Raymond Caelen, Phyllis Pilgrim, Noah Rolland; Skylonda Fitness Retreat: Tomas Byrna, Sue Chapman, Dixon Collins, Kathy Collins, Neal Johnson; The Spa at the Houstonian: Kathy Driscoll, Michelle Brookins, Mickie McIntyre-Tubbs; Spa Grande at Grand Wailea Resort: Darryll Leiman.

Many thanks also to the following spa experts for their tremendous experience and perspective: Jonathan Paul De Vierville, Lisa Dobloug, Mary Hannigan, Ginny Lopis, Kim Marshall, Erika Miller, Patricia Monteson, Sylvia Sepielli, Frank van Putten, and Alan Wayler. Special thanks to ISPA (International Spa and Fitness Association) for permission to use recipes from their member spas, the ISPA Collaboration.

Thank you, as well, to those who gave time and energy, prepared food and donated houses, contributing to the book's photographs in a major way: Chef Nick Morfogen and the staff of Aspen's Ajax Tavern; manager Walt Harris and the staff of Aspen's Syzygy restaurant; Andy DiSabatino, Muffy DiSabatino, John Elkhorn and Susan Kaye, Diane Rutgers, Bill Sharp, Pat Sharp, and Kim Sheelar. A very special thanks to Beth and Bill O'Donnell.

And, of course, much gratitude to our intrepid models: Sophia Anastasia, Tricia Atkinson, Bridget Birrfelder, Mary Carrabba, Leslie Christenson, JoAnn Connington, Lisa Feldman, Terri Hart, Ben Herman, Robert Jensen, Susan Kaye, Laura MacDougall, Melanie Malone, Moorea the dog, Robert Novak, Klaus Obermeyer, Julie Oldham, Brooke Peterson, Ivan Petkov, Sharon Petkov, Terri Roe, Denise Searle, Susan Walker, Chip Whipple, Lynne Whipple, and Ed Zane.

Thanks and bon appetit to those who tested and tasted the recipes in the book: Gina Berko, Jenny Cook, Sue Dirkes, Carolyn Harder, Susan Kaye, Susan Marx, Beth O'Donnell, David Roth, Diane Rutgers, Gayle Schwartz, Denise Searle, Jill Sheeley, Cindy Sullivan, Rudy Vavra, Ellen Walbert, and Lynne Whipple.

We especially want to thank Jill Uris for so wonderfully capturing the spa life in her photographs, and Suzanne De Galan, our editor, for her insightful guidance and steady encouragement.

Last, but not least, appreciation and much love go to our husbands, Brooke Peterson and Tim Sullivan, for the support, understanding and sense of humor they maintained during the months *The Spa Life at Home* was being created in *our* homes.

The Spa Life at home

INTRODUCTION

In these stressful times, more and more of us are searching for ways to achieve balance in our lives. At times it may seem like an impossible dream, yet this desire for balance is driving many of us to rearrange our priorities. We know that lifestyle plays a major role in the well-being we seek. The way we eat, exercise and cope with stress is at the core of a healthy, balanced life. But knowledge isn't always enough. Most of us need a little help to make and keep the commitments that can turn our lives around.

Increasingly, people are turning to spas for that help. Twenty years ago, there were only thirty spas in the United States. Today, there are more than 250 destination retreats and spas at vacation resorts and hotels. The number of day spas is rapidly increasing as well. No longer just places where the rich go to lose a few pounds and enjoy a little pampering, spas in this country are becoming schools for balanced living and the preventive medicine centers of our time.

At spas, you get your body moving, learn to eat well and let go of accumulated tension. In the process you may discover—perhaps for the first time in your life—the connection between mind and body, and that neglecting one will hurt the other. After a few days or a week at a spa, you often feel a renewed sense of well-being, and so gather the momentum needed to produce more lasting change.

But spa visits are temporary. Even if you come home determined to implement change in your life, it may be hard to motivate yourself to exercise, eat well and take time to relax. *The Spa Life at Home* was written for those of you looking for ongoing ways to include all the elements of healthful living in your day while balancing family, jobs and other responsibilities. This book is a blueprint for building that special spa synergy—the combination of physical activity, a healthful diet, body care and relaxation—that leads to a better quality of life. Think of it as your guide to daily living.

To give you insight into the ways spas encourage lifestyle change, we've gathered advice from the most respected experts on spas in the country. Here is one-stop spa shopping, a compilation of philosophies, information, recipes, tips and inspiration. Some of the ideas in these pages will be familiar, but perhaps not in this context. We've combined them in a way that reflects the spa vision of balance and given you a framework for living the spa life at home.

We have structured the book to mirror a typical day you might spend at a destination spa. During a week at one of these classic retreats, you would probably begin each day by rising early and walking or stretching before breakfast, then spend the morning exercising. After lunch come body treatments, then a snack and relaxation before dinner. To evoke the rhythm of a spa day, the book is divided into eight chapters that cover morning wake-up, breakfast, fitness, lunch, beauty and body, snack, rest and relaxation and dinner. While schedules will vary, these are the basic elements of a spa day and the ones to include in a spa life at home.

We are not suggesting that you live every day as though you were at a spa. That would be impossible. A spa vacation is exactly that: a rest from work, family, household chores and community obligations. At home it may be difficult to find ways to fit in the various elements of the spa life along with everything else you do in a day. That's why, in each chapter, we have addressed the issues that probably make it hardest for you to exercise regularly, make your meals more healthful and take time to nurture yourself. There's no magic formula. We have, however, included the best advice we could find from spas to help you find ways and reasons to try.

The link between healthful living, disease prevention and longevity may or may not be addressed directly at spas, but it is at the heart of their overall philosophy. Although the connection is implied here, this book is not an appropriate forum for discussing scientific research. Like any general guidance, the information in *The Spa Life at Home* is not targeted to any one individual's health concerns. For information on the connections between lifestyle and specific health conditions, there are many excellent sources available today. Also, if you are worried about trying any of the techniques suggested in this book, consult your personal physician.

There are many ways to use this book. If you are having trouble dealing with stress or getting started on an exercise program, for example, study the chapters dealing with those specific issues. Keep in mind, however, that diet, fitness and relaxation interconnect and overlap. Improvement in one area may lead to unexpected success in another, and you may find the answers you seek in places you don't expect to find them.

It's also possible to browse through the book and note tips, recipes or exercises that are especially appealing. Implement them one at a time, in a way that feels most natural. Or select the most tempting techniques and suggestions and design a spa weekend for you and your friends. In that case, you'll want to read the book from beginning to end to ensure that your program is as rich and textured as one at a spa.

The Spa Life at Home does not suggest that there is only one right way to live. It does not spell out a minute-by-minute or day-by-day routine. There's no universal exercise prescription here. Even the healthful, low-fat recipes do not include measurements of calories or fat grams. Ultimately, health is not a matter of numbers, nor is it about deprivation or compulsion. Balanced living has to be what works best for you. We have suggested many alternatives, but in the long run, you are the one who must decide how much exercise is right for you, what kinds and amounts of foods you should eat to give you energy without adding weight, and what is the best way for you to deal with stress. This book can give you ideas and inspiration, but the balance comes in the living.

Above all, we hope *The Spa Life at Home* will help you see that health is about living each day with pleasure, energy and enthusiasm. Vitality is a natural state and one that can be recaptured day by day. Finding balance is a process that continues forever. The spa life is a journey, not a destination.

GREET THE DAY

Dawn is just beginning to break. It may still be dark outside, but at spas all over the country, people are beginning to wake up. Regardless of the spa's philosophy, five to seven in the morning is prime time for rising and engaging in some prebreakfast activity. When the early-morning call is sounded, you may be tempted to roll over and ignore it, particularly if it is early in your spa stay. Those who have already spent a few days rising early know the benefits. They know that a morning stretch is one of the best ways to start the day, and that a morning walk leaves the body energized and refreshed for hours to come. They know how camaraderie is built on early-morning hikes, and how nature can make friends of the most opposite personalities. So, even though you may want to sleep another couple of hours, you won't. Throw the covers off and pull on the sweats. Greet the day with optimism. Start by doing something that makes you feel better about yourself. Rising early is a way of life at spas everywhere.

Early to bed, early to rise . . . you've heard the saying a million times, but at spas it's one that's believed almost universally. At a spa, it isn't difficult to get into such a routine. After a day of exercise, a massage, a little pampering and a healthful, early dinner, almost no one has trouble drifting off to sleep by nine or ten o'clock. A good night's deep sleep makes it much easier to face the dawn with enough energy for a hike or a yoga class.

At home your situation may be slightly different. Whether it's work, kids or a visiting relative, something often will keep you up late or feeling so stressed you have trouble falling asleep at all. You may be one of the millions of sleep-deprived Americans struggling to find enough hours in the day to get everything done, let alone get to bed early enough to rise before dawn. Sometimes you feel like you'd clean out your bank account for an extra hour or two of sleep, and sometimes sleep really is what you need more than anything else. But if you want to make a lifestyle change, start by using those early-morning hours for something other than throwing on your clothes and eating a mad-dash breakfast before rushing out of the house. You will be rewarded in ways you haven't even considered.

At a spa you have the benefit of knowing that everyone else is rising early too, and sometimes that collective energy alone can be enough to get you started. At home you may have to schedule dinners or meetings earlier to allow yourself to get to bed earlier. Convince your partner to give early rising a try as well. Until you get into the habit, you'll need to rely on friends or family to help you get up for early walks, stretching or yoga. Knowing that someone is waiting for you at the park can be all the incentive you need to drag yourself out of bed.

Eventually, it will get easier. You may lose an hour or two of sleep at first until your body adjusts and you are able to get to sleep earlier. Eventually, though, your body will attune itself to the natural cycle of rising with the sun and going to sleep soon after dark. Allowing yourself to do what comes naturally will promote the deep sleep that leaves you completely rested and allows you to awaken with the dawn, more refreshed and alert.

Now that you're up, the options of what to do with that extra time are bountiful. American spas, almost without exception, encourage guests to start the day with a thirty- to sixty-minute walk before breakfast. Inherited from European spas, this tradition of "body hardening"—brisk air on the face and feet touching the ground—has long been considered one of the best ways to start the day.

This concept works equally well at home. Walking is one activity nearly everyone can do regardless of fitness level. It doesn't have to be vigorous, either. Since your body is just waking up, treat it gently. Begin with a few pre-walk stretches and start slowly, picking up the pace as you feel ready. Go slow enough to talk easily to your neighbor without feeling breathless. Make the walk enjoyable, and take time to notice the world around you.

At a spa, conversing with a friend on an early-morning walk is the perfect way to promote camaraderie. Your walk can have the same effect at home with friends and family and may become the one time in your day when you can have a real conversation. Maybe it's because you're together in nature, maybe it's because you're spending quiet time with someone before the stress of the day sets in, but you'll be amazed at the connections you can develop with others on a trail or even just circling the neighborhood. At three in the afternoon, when all is in chaos, you'll look back on that time as one of the best of your day.

The other real bonus to walking is that it can be done anywhere, in any climate, on manmade or natural terrain. Wherever you live, from New York City to Omaha, there's someplace nearby where you can walk. If you like, look at it as a form of sightseeing. At Norwich Inn and Spa in Norwich, Connecticut, for example, guests on their morning walks tour the property, getting a workout and a view of the old New England estate at the same time. At the Heartland Spa in Gilman, Illinois, and the New Age Spa in Neversink, New York, early risers stroll down country roads. At Ihilani Resort and Spa on Oahu, Hawaii, and the Anara Spa at the Hyatt Regency on Kauai, Hawaii, guests walk along paved paths that offer ocean panoramas, while at the Doral Golf Resort and Spa in Miami, guests wind their way through the golf course.

Spas generally have a large amount of acreage at their disposal and are able to offer a variety of walks and hikes, from flat trails winding through groomed terrain to ones that rise and twist through challenging mountain wilderness. Often you have the option to start with easy walks and move to tougher routes as your fitness level improves. At Canyon Ranch in Tucson, for example, guests get a choice of one-, two-, three-, four- and eight-mile walks and hikes through the Sonoran Desert.

At home, you may not have the same variety of choices and the nearest wilderness may be miles away, but you can certainly find a park or a golf course or even a network of sidewalks that can substitute. All it takes is a little creativity to vary the pace and distance as your fitness level improves. Go faster, look for hills, do more loops, even climb stairs outside if you don't have other more natural options.

This walk may be your only chance to get outside all day long—and you should take advantage of it.

Sometimes early morning is the only time the weather allows you to be outside. In climates like those of Arizona and Utah, where summertime temperatures can top 100 degrees, outdoor activity aside from swimming is nearly intolerable except in the early morning. The desert is no place to find yourself outdoors in midday in July or August. That's why, in places like Miraval Life in Balance in Tucson and Rancho La Puerta in Baja, California, most of the walking and hiking takes place in the early morning.

If walking just doesn't work for you, there are other ways to take advantage of early hours. The Golden Door, in Escondido, California, for example, teaches journal writing as a wake-up exercise for the mind. It's a way to take advantage of the creative transition time between dark and light, sleep and awake, that usually gets lost in the attempt to grab a few more minutes of sleep or the craziness of morning activities. In fact, writing in a journal is a form of meditation. Immediately upon waking, reach for the journal and write down anything that comes to mind—dreams, goals for the day, problems and feelings. It's a wonderful, cathartic exercise, and you'll be surprised at what you come up with before the day has intruded on your thoughts.

Almost every spa offers traditional morning stretch classes or the integrated mind-body methods of yoga and t'ai chi as wake-up options. With their specific poses or slow, sustained movements, these activities are superb ways of shaking off morning stiffness and focusing your mind. If you like waking up

flowing and defog the mind. Depending on where you live, there may be an early-morning stretch or yoga class on television. Or you may prefer to improvise your own routine based on how you feel from day to day.

However you choose to start the day, there are ample reasons to do something in the morning. Moving your muscles immediately upon rising can increase your metabolism, boost your energy level and lift your mood. It can even help with weight maintenance. You prepare your body and clear your mind for the coming day and give yourself a head start on living it well.

Finally, you can be sure that whatever you commit to do first thing in the morning will get done rather than be lost in the day's demands. How many times have you told yourself you'll take a walk when you get home from work and then found a reason not to? The excuses pile up until a month or a year has passed and you still have done nothing about saving some time for yourself. If you can adjust your schedule so that you have half an hour to an hour in the morning, it will be much easier to avoid procrastination.

> **"Get the body moving, and the mind will follow."**
> Sylvia Sepielli, owner, Sylvia Resorts and Spas

slowly or particularly cherish a quiet time all to yourself in the morning, you may like these gentle activities better than any other wake-up option. Even fifteen minutes of mild t'ai chi, yoga or stretching can help prepare your body for the day ahead.

Mild is the operative word here. At spas, the yoga or stretching done early in the morning is totally different from the more athletic versions you may try later in the day. Instead of pushing your muscles to the limit, the idea upon waking is to loosen up by breathing deeply and paying close attention to body sensations. Imagine your dog or cat stretching after waking from a nap. That's the same kind of easy, natural movement you want in the morning—just enough exertion to get energy

Remember, your morning wake-up routine doesn't have to be complicated or time-consuming. Just taking a little time to wake up mentally and physically—by stretching, taking a short walk, writing in a journal—before moving full speed into life's daily complications is your first step toward a more productive and satisfying life.

Walking to Start Your Day

Hailed as nature's first exercise, walking is both the most respected and the most disrespected of modern workouts. As something anyone with two feet can do regardless of fitness level, it is often dismissed as too simple or easy to be of any value. Nothing is further from the truth. Walking at any level tones muscles, helps maintain weight, reduces stress, provides a perfect atmosphere for introspection or, conversely, for social activity, and provides an all-around, low-impact workout. Just as important, for those who do it regularly, it can lead to or supplement more intense exercise.

As an early-morning wake-up, walking can't be beat. If you like to wake up slowly you might use the walking time for quiet meditation, as a way to open up to the day. If you prefer a little more action in the morning you can elevate the pace to levels that burn more calories and boost aerobic fitness. At any level, walking is a versatile, effective way to start the day any time of the year, in almost any environment. By taking it at your own pace and using it as the foundation of your physical fitness regime, you should be able to continue walking into very old age.

Walking clinics at many spas address the basic challenge of walking as a workout: how to pick up the pace to challenge the heart and lungs without straining and stressing your joints and muscles. Techniques and lingo may vary, but some fundamentals apply.

Before You Begin Invest in a good pair of walking shoes. The market has exploded in the past few years with shoes designed for the rolling gait of walking, so you should have no trouble finding a comfortable, good-fitting pair. The usual criteria apply: Try them on with the socks you intend to wear, and be sure there's a thumb's-width space between the end of the shoe and your toes and that the heel fits snugly, with little slippage.

Posture Walking comfortably starts with posture. Keep your head in a neutral position, with your chin parallel to the ground and your shoulders down and relaxed. Find a stride length that lets you keep this upright and relaxed stance. Let your arms swing naturally in opposition to your stride. Aim for a smooth, fluid gait and remember to breathe. On uphills, maintain your speed by shortening your stride. On downhills, soften your knees to decrease impact. Light stretching after your workout—especially for calves, fronts and backs of thighs and shoulders—will help keep muscles loose and your gait smooth.

Putting in the Time At first don't worry about speed. Frequency and duration are more important than intensity. If you are a beginning walker, start by setting a goal of fifteen to twenty minutes, or an amount of time you can walk without exhausting yourself. Increase your distance by no more than half a mile per week until you can complete three miles. You should find yourself improving rapidly. Ideally, you should walk at least four times a week, upping the frequency to as much as seven days a week if you have weight to lose. Unlike many other physical activities, walking is fine to do on a daily basis.

Speeding Up For greater aerobic challenge, pick up the pace until you can walk a mile in fourteen to eighteen minutes. To do this, you will need to lean forward a bit from your ankles, shorten your stride and roll through your foot from ball to heel on each step. Don't bend forward at the waist, which strains the back and hampers breathing, or take oversized strides. Bend your arms as they swing so they don't drag on your momentum; keep your elbows at about ninety degrees. Make sure your forward swing doesn't cross your chest or swing higher than your shoulders.

Some walkers like to push their limits, reaching twelve-minute miles or faster. At this level, you get the aerobic intensity of running without the impact on joints. With greater speed, posture and technique become even more important. As you swing your arms, keep them close to your body, almost hugging your sides. Keep your hands in a loose fist, and don't let them swing back farther than your waist. Keep your feet moving alongside an imaginary straight line, almost as if you were walking a tightrope, and let your hips rotate in a natural motion. Your power will come from the toe action of the rear foot as it propels you forward.

By continuing to concentrate on posture, rhythm and speed, your movements should become synchronized until you begin to feel relaxed at any pace. As your fitness level improves, you'll be able to roll along for miles. You'll face the rest of the day with a clear mind, extra energy and a better overall attitude.

A Mind-Calming Meditation Walk

There's no question that a morning walk can be a great time to bond with friends and family while getting some outdoor exercise. But once in awhile, break the routine and try something different. Instead of chatting your way up a mountain or along a walking trail, be silent and use the time for quiet contemplation.

Walks like this, based on meditation techniques, are practiced at Rancho La Puerta and Miraval Life in Balance. By focusing on your body and your surroundings as you walk—the sound of your footsteps, the feel of your breath and the sights of nature—these walks help you learn to be fully present in the moment instead of ruminating about the past or future or spending so much time talking to fellow walkers that you take no notice of what's happening around you.

Until you try, you may not realize how difficult it can be to keep your thoughts from straying to problems at work, what you want for breakfast or something you wish you hadn't said or done. Don't give up. Everyone's mind is naturally restless, and whenever you notice your thoughts have wandered, simply return your attention to your breathing, your surroundings or whatever focus you have chosen. Training your attention comes only through practice. Just by making the attempt, you will find your mind becoming more clear and the mental chatter diminishing. The path you walk every day may begin to look very different as you notice details for the first time. Use these ideas to get started:

Pick a place to walk that's secure and relatively free of distraction. This way you'll be able to turn your full concentration to whatever you choose to contemplate. Don't talk. Open yourself to the surroundings.

(continued on page 12)

(continued from page 11)

Walk slowly. This is not the time to worry about your target heart rate. A snail's pace isn't necessary, but go slow enough that you can breathe easily. On this walk, distance is not your goal.

Be aware of each step you take. If you find your mind beginning to wander, bring your attention back to your footfall. If you prefer, pay attention to the way your chest rises and falls as you breathe.

Stop a few times along the way to notice what's around you. What are the sounds, smells and sights?

For variation, imagine that you are standing in one place, as though on a treadmill, and that the world is moving past you.

Pay attention to how you feel at the end of the walk. Are you calmer? Can you recall that state of mind throughout the rest of the day?

Morning Stretch: Mobilizing Your Body

Even if there's time for nothing else, a short morning stretch can do wonders toward getting your body ready for the day. The chronic tension that tends to build throughout the day can compound the normal stiffness you feel when you first get out of bed. A slow, steady wake-up of the joints and muscles, just enough to get energy flowing, can make you feel more supple and relaxed all day.

Even when time is short, be sure to savor each move. Pushing stiff muscles won't do a bit of good. Forcing your body into uncomfortable positions may only make you tighter or, worse, cause injuries. Better to do one or two stretches very slowly than to rush through ten. By warming up gradually, keeping motions small and paying close attention to what your body is telling you, you'll know exactly how far to stretch.

Maintain this attitude as you design your morning wake-up from the multitude of possible stretching exercises and routines you can learn in classes and from books and videos. Soon, you'll learn which of them your body needs and responds to best. Whichever you decide to do, here are some pointers from the morning stretch class at Skylonda Fitness Retreat in Woodside, California.

Maintain the mood. *Each morning, guests virtually roll out of bed into the stretching studio and onto exercise mats. You can do the same at home by keeping a mat or rug handy in your bedroom or nearby closet. Keep the lights off so*

you can enjoy the dawn. Don't turn on the television or radio, unless, of course, you're tuning in
to an early-morning stretch or yoga show. Wear
loose-fitting clothes for comfort, and, most
important, take your time.

▍ **Use your breath.** *Breathing properly can help
with every stretch you make and leave you energized and exhilarated when you're done. Inhaling deeply allows fresh oxygen to move into your
muscles, and a full exhale allows carbon dioxide*

to leave. *The natural rhythm of your breath can
serve as your metronome. Move into the stretch as
you inhale and relax or deepen into it as you
exhale. Let yourself respond spontaneously.
Yawns, sighs and even groans are natural
responses as tensions release. They also help to get
air flowing.*

▍ **Focus your attention.** *When someone tells
you to "breathe into" a part of your body, they
are telling you to focus your attention on that*

spot. Because of the link between the mind and muscles, sometimes using imagination to picture the release of tightness is what it takes to relax into the day. As you inhale, imagine your breath filling an area of your body. On exhaling, picture tension flowing out. When you combine breathing and mental focus this way, it has a calming and energizing effect at the same time. Even the most basic stretches will let you breathe life back into your body every morning.

The Art of Journal Writing

By placing a pad and pencil beside your bed at night and reaching for it immediately upon opening your eyes in the morning, you may be able to take advantage of a very creative period of the day. Spas are beginning to recognize the potential in early-morning journal writing. Some are even teaching their guests journaling techniques for gaining insight into themselves.

There are many reasons early morning is considered prime time for journal writing. Cleared from the clutter of the previous day and not yet distracted by the one ahead, your mind is better able to focus and your thoughts to flow into words. Especially if you have children, early morning may be the only time in the day when you can be alone with your thoughts.

Whenever you choose to do it, journal writing is a wonderful way to vent feelings, look more closely at interpersonal conflicts and gain insight into what is most important in your life. Sometimes just writing about pain can help you let go of it.

For many people, getting started is the hardest part. Instructors at the Golden Door suggests asking yourself questions, then writing down the answers that come spontaneously to mind. Ask yourself what is changing or ending in your life, or what the next steps are that you need to take to give yourself a greater sense of well-being.

You may find it easier to get started by writing about a fantasy day—the best day you've ever had or can imagine having in your life. Make a list of every wonderful thing you wish would happen in a twenty-four-hour period, then use this list as a catalyst. Reflect on how many of those wonderful things are occurring in your life right now. If the answer is not many, try to come up with ways you could begin to shift the balance.

There really is no right or wrong way to keep a journal. You don't have to be Jane Austen or even worry about spelling and grammar if that hampers your ability to write freely. You may choose to write purely as a means of letting go. (Some people go so far as to burn their journals after filling the pages.)

You may want to ignore the lines and write all over the page, draw pictures or cut out cartoons or quotations and add them as you go. Date entries and use your journal to chronicle your life. You can actually write your own history and look back from year to year to discover how your thoughts and feelings have changed. Once you start, you may find that journal writing becomes not only an early-morning exercise but a cathartic experience that opens up a whole new inner world.

Reality Check

Put First Things First

If there's never enough time in your day, do what's most important to you first. Whether it's exercising, getting outside or simply spending some quiet time alone, do it as soon as you wake up. That way, there's little chance you will forget or run out of time to do it. Putting first things first is one of the simplest steps you can take toward creating better balance in your life.

FUEL FOR THE MORNING

The morning is still young, and you've already finished your wake-up walk or stretch. You're alert, ready to face the day and more than ready for breakfast. At some spas, you'll head for the dining room with your walking or hiking companions to savor the first meal of the day. Often it's served buffet-style, sometimes à la carte, and it's a social affair, a time to compare notes on the classes you've chosen for the morning. At other spas, breakfast is a time to be alone to reflect on the day ahead. It's served in your room, on a beautiful tray along with your schedule for the rest of the day. Either way, the early exercise has left you hungry and more than ready to break your fast from the night before.

As the first meal of the day, breakfast at a spa boosts your energy level and then keeps it on an even keel throughout the morning. It supplies the fuel you need for physical stamina and mental sharpness throughout the day, no matter what you have planned. At spas, no one would even consider missing breakfast. If you do at home, you set yourself up for fatigue and irritability. By mid-morning you're likely to feel slow and unfocused. If you're trying to lose weight, the strategy of saving calories by forgoing breakfast can backfire. Mid-morning hunger pangs send you running to grab anything in sight.

Comprising one-quarter to one-third of all the food eaten in a day, spa breakfasts are substantial enough to provide the stamina to last the morning, but light enough to stave off sluggishness. Typically, spas favor grains and fruit for breakfast, complemented by small amounts of milk, yogurt and eggs. You might find homemade granola with skim milk and a scattering of blackberries along with a couple of small, chewy bran muffins, or oat-bran pancakes topped with warm apple butter or, perhaps, an egg-white omelette with spinach, sun-dried tomatoes and freshly picked herbs, a side of whole-grain toast and a peeled orange. A healthful breakfast, whether it's simple or elaborate, should provide you with enough energy and brain food to get you through the morning feeling strong and alert.

If you rarely feel hungry in the morning, eating even a small amount may have a real impact on how you feel the rest of the day. If you absolutely can't face a big breakfast in one sitting, try spreading it out over the morning in a couple of mini-meals. Have a piece of fruit after rising and then eat a muffin or a bagel mid-morning. The point is to *eat something* in the morning so you can make it to lunch without feeling famished. If you aren't starving at lunchtime, you'll be less likely to overeat, something to keep in mind if you're trying to lose weight.

In fact, going hungry is never a good idea. Spa nutritionists advocate keeping your energy at a steady level throughout the day by eating three meals and perhaps a snack or two. This may come as a surprise if you've always thought of spas as places to go to starve off excess pounds with scanty diets. Your notion may be that healthful eating, at the very least, means being deprived and constantly having to say "no." Nothing could be further from the truth.

At spas, the food is delicious, imaginative and extremely satisfying. Creative chefs translate the ideals of healthful eating into delectable, filling dishes that are beautifully presented. At the Greenhouse in Arlington, Texas, for example, you get as many as ten options each morning, including golden waffles with strawberry compote and berries or steaming old-fashioned oatmeal with skim milk and raisins, and your meal is waiting in your room on a silver tray after a

> ## "We've learned how to starve. Now we need to learn how to eat."
> Alan Wayler, executive director, Green Mountain at Fox Run

walk. At the Bonaventure Resort and Spa in Fort Lauderdale, Florida, egg-white omelettes are flavored with wild mushrooms, shallots and fresh herbs, while a perfect pile of silver-dollar-sized pancakes comes sweetened with warm peach conserve. With a few simple touches, any meal you cook at home can be as appetizing as the food at the most gourmet spas.

What you learn at a spa is a sensible, positive approach to lifelong eating. Simply put, that means cutting back on fat, sugar and salt, but not avoiding them entirely, and eating more whole grains, lean meats, fruits and vegetables. At home, all your favorite dishes can easily be made more healthful and still retain every bit of flavor. Spa recipes, for example, are simple to follow, and substitutions for fat and sugar generally have little impact on taste. If you don't mention it, your family may never even notice you used applesauce in place of sugar or skim milk instead of whole.

Learning to make low-fat versions of your favorite foods—muffins, pancakes, French toast—is one of the easiest ways to introduce spa living at home. Even traditionally high-fat dishes such as sausage and hash browns can be made in low-fat versions by substituting turkey for beef and making a defatted version of "home fries," as they do at the Cooper Aerobics Center in Dallas. If hearty Sunday breakfasts have always been a tradition in your family, there's no need to throw out your mother's recipes or even your favorite cookbook. Simply follow some suggestions made by spas for ways to cut the fat, make healthful substitutions and then indulge in the same delicious breakfasts you've always enjoyed.

It's important to realize, however, that improving your diet is not just a matter of removing ingredients from recipes but of adding foods that you need in abundance every single day. The dietary balance spas have been achieving for years is now reflected in U.S. government guidelines for a healthful diet: very little fat and sugar; a moderate amount of milk and dairy products, meat, nuts, beans and eggs; and lots of fruits, vegetables and grains. The guidelines are presented in the form of a food pyramid that suggests specific portions of the different kinds of food you need to eat each day. Once you begin following these recommendations, you'll be well on your way to eating spa-style.

By developing a good eye for nutritious choices, you'll also have no trouble facing any breakfast or brunch buffet in the world. At spas such as Rancho La Puerta in Baja, California, Lake Austin Spa Resort in Austin, Texas, Miraval Life in Balance in Tucson and Canyon Ranch in Tucson, you choose items ranging from hot and cold cereals to a variety of fresh and dried fruits, low-fat yogurt, cottage cheese, boiled eggs, toast, muffins, omelettes, crepes, pancakes and waffles. With so many choices, you rarely get bored and you give your body the widest range of energy-supplying nutrients. At spas, most buffet items are low fat and nutrition-oriented, so it's hard to make an unhealthful choice. Most restaurant buffets, however, won't have filtered out menu items with high fat and heavy sugar content, and you'll have to recall the pyramid guidelines to make the best choices.

The pyramid can even help when you must

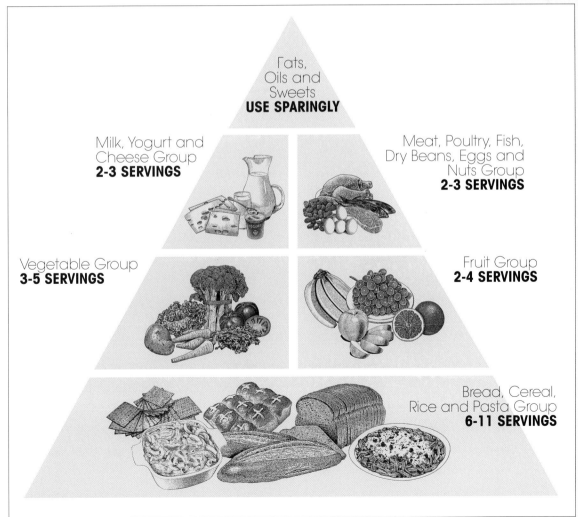

Fats,
Oils and
Sweets
USE SPARINGLY

Milk, Yogurt and
Cheese Group
2-3 SERVINGS

Meat, Poultry, Fish,
Dry Beans, Eggs and
Nuts Group
2-3 SERVINGS

Vegetable Group
3-5 SERVINGS

Fruit Group
2-4 SERVINGS

Bread, Cereal,
Rice and Pasta Group
6-11 SERVINGS

eat breakfast on the run. Instead of grabbing for a doughnut, sweet roll or other typical breakfast treat, try a teaspoon of peanut butter on a bagel, half a cup of cottage cheese and an apple or a breakfast smoothie made with yogurt and bananas. All contain many necessary nutrients, have few empty calories and can easily be thrown together when time is short.

Breakfast, like all meals, should also be about *taking time*—to replenish your body but also to be alone, writing in your journal or organizing your day. You may prefer to make it a social occasion that you spend with family before everyone heads in separate directions. If you like the idea of making breakfast a ritual but you simply don't have the time for elaborate preparation, try planning menus ahead of time. Many breakfast foods, including pancakes, waffles and bread, can be frozen and easily thawed in the morning.

If mornings in your home are completely frantic, there may be no time to set a tray, let alone make it beautiful. If you're the last one to leave in the morning, wait until everyone is gone to lay out a tray for yourself and enjoy a few minutes of quiet before your day begins. If this isn't practical, try keeping a tray at the office and carrying something with you that you can set out at work and enjoy at your desk. By using a little creativity, you can make breakfast a much more civilized and appealing affair.

However it works best for you, breaking the fast in the morning is as important as anything else you do in the day. Give yourself a positive nutritional head start in the morning, and you'll be on the path to healthful eating all day long.

The Fundamentals of Breakfast

Long before it became fashionable, spas were serving a diet rich in grains, fruits and vegetables and low in fat and sugar. This way of eating reflects a philosophy at the heart of spa cuisine, no matter how much individual spa styles differ.

A similar diet, represented by the widely distributed food pyramid, is now being promoted by the federal government as the most healthful way to eat. At the tip of the pyramid, or its smallest point, are fats, sweets and oils, all foods to eat sparingly. The broad base includes grains, breads and cereals, which should make up the bulk of your diet. Just above grains are fruits and vegetables, more foods to eat in abundance, while above them and just below the tip of the pyramid are dairy products and meat, poultry, fish, beans, eggs and nuts, foods you'll want to eat in moderation and in low-fat and lean versions whenever possible.

By keeping the pyramid in mind at breakfast, you should be able to make more healthful choices, whether you're eating at a buffet, ordering off a menu or cooking at home. You will know, for instance, that you should choose a bowl of cereal and a side of toast over a cheese omelette, and that blackberries or raisins in place of sugar will enhance your oatmeal with vitamins and nutrients, while using skim milk instead of whole is a good way to reduce fat.

The pyramid also provides the suggested number of servings of foods from each food group that you should eat each day. Keep in mind that the range of suggested servings is wide to accommodate everyone from inactive women, who need to eat the least, to very active men, who need to eat the most. Judge your own needs accordingly.

Consider typical breakfast options: cereals and breads, fruits, eggs, milk. The guidelines recommend that you have between six and eleven servings each day of bread and grains. That sounds like a lot, until you consider that one serving is only one slice of bread, one-half cup of cooked cereal or one ounce of ready-to-eat cereal. You might be getting all the grains you need in an entire day just by having a large bowl of oatmeal and a couple of pieces of toast.

The same is true for the other food groups. For example, the guidelines recommend that you have two to four servings of fruit each day. Just one whole piece of fruit, three-quarters of a cup of juice or one-half cup of dried fruit makes up a serving. If you drink a small glass of juice with breakfast and add a handful of raisins or berries to your cereal, you are well on your way to having all the fruit recommended for an entire day.

Moving up the pyramid, you find that the recommendations for low-fat milk, yogurt and cheese are two to three servings a day, and that one cup of skim milk or yogurt or one and a half ounces of cheese comprise a serving. Milk on your cereal or a fruit and yogurt smoothie are good, filling ways to get dairy products at breakfast. On the other hand, aficionados of cheese omelettes and bagels and cream cheese can overdose at one meal. The same holds true for those who love eggs and bacon. The recommendation is that you have no more than

two to three servings a day of eggs and meat combined, or a total of only five to seven ounces. When you realize that one egg is the equivalent of an ounce, you can see that the totals add up quickly.

By eating mostly grains and fruits at breakfast, as you do at spas, and adding a moderate amount of milk or even an egg when desired, you'll be surprised at how much you can eat and how satisfying your meals can be. For example, two pieces of toast plus a cup of yogurt whipped up in a blender with a banana and mango is not only delicious but should keep you full till lunch. A cup of oatmeal with one-half cup of skim milk and a handful of dried currants, a boiled egg and a glass of orange juice is a sizable breakfast by most standards. Pancakes, waffles, granola and muffins are equally acceptable breakfast items that meet pyramid standards as long as you choose low-fat versions, use little or no butter and opt for fruit over syrup, sugar or jam.

The pyramid does not provide a rigid formula you need to follow exactly. It was designed to accommodate a broad population, and you'll have to find the foods and amounts that work best for you. Simply consider the pyramid a framework for healthful eating, one that can help you formulate a personal eating style for reaching and maintaining your desired weight and keeping your energy level high.

■ The Facts on Fiber

Breakfast provides a particularly good opportunity to get fiber into your diet, since many cereals, fruits and breads are rich in fiber. Fiber comes only from plant foods such as fruits, vegetables and whole grains. It makes up the bulk that moves food through the digestive tract more smoothly and eases the digestive process.

Fiber is the secret behind many successful spa dishes—food that is full of flavor, pleasurable to eat and very filling without much fat. Foods that have a lot of fiber generally take longer to eat because they are denser. In addition, all the bulk fills you up faster and stays in your system longer, so you don't feel hungry again soon after a meal. Since your appetite is sated, you're able to do with less food.

For all these reasons, it's important to eat a variety of fiber-rich foods every day. This shouldn't be difficult, since fiber comprises a large part of some of the best-tasting foods around. For breakfast, good choices are melons, pears, blueberries, strawberries, kiwis, oranges and other fruits; whole-grain breads and muffins; and many popular morning cereals.

If you read the labels on the sides of cereal boxes, you should be able to determine pretty quickly which of your favorites are high in fiber. Experts recommend 25 grams of fiber for those on a diet of 2,000 calories per day (some believe up to twice that much fiber is good for your health). Eating as little as half a cup of bran cereal in the morning will give you 50 percent of that daily allotment. If you don't like the taste of high-fiber cereal "straight," try sprinkling it on oatmeal or yogurt, or mix it into a smoothie. A note of caution: To avoid bloating, gas and even constipation, add fiber to your diet slowly, so your body can adjust, and be sure to drink lots of water throughout the day.

Here are some other tips on ways to add more fiber to your diet:

▌ *Eat raw or slightly cooked vegetables instead of vegetables that have been cooked for a long time. When possible, eat skins and edible stalks.*

▌ *Eat fresh and dried fruit instead of canned fruit or fruit juice. Eat edible skin and membranes.*

▌ *Eat pastas and breads made with whole-grain or whole-wheat flour instead of white, and brown rice instead of white rice.*

▌ *Eat oatmeal or whole-grain cereal instead of creamed cereals.*

▌ Eating Out, Spa-Style

Some people absolutely love eating out in the mornings. If you're one of them, remember that even in a restaurant, it's possible to keep breakfast healthful and nutritious. Most restaurants these days are happy to custom-prepare your meal. If you want an omelette, for example, but don't want to eat the daily special made with three whole eggs and a filling of ham and cheese, ask if the chef will make yours of egg whites, or with one whole egg and two whites. You probably won't be able to tell the difference, and it's not difficult for the kitchen to comply. Instead of cheese and ham, choose fillings such as spinach, tomatoes and mushrooms, or ask for some sautéed vegetables topped off with salsa. You'll get a well-rounded meal full of nutrients and fiber and still have the eggs you wanted for breakfast.

If pancakes or waffles are more to your taste, ask for jelly or applesauce instead of sugary syrup and melted butter. Use low-fat or skim milk on your cereal, and sweeten it with berries or bananas. Ask for English muffins, bagels and toast dry so the chef won't butter them in the kitchen and leave you with no options. Choose whole-wheat or multigrain over white bread, and avoid buttery croissants. These are simple requests for restaurants to accommodate. By adapting these modifications, you'll make a big difference in the fat and calorie content of your next breakfast out.

It's also important to keep an eye on the size of your servings. A muffin may be full of grains and fiber but high in calories and fat as well. Just because food is nutritious doesn't mean you can eat it in unlimited quantities. Buffets can be especially tricky. Instead of sampling a little of everything, try taking only two or three items and go back for seconds only if you are still hungry after eating those.

The same is true when ordering off the menu. Order modestly at the beginning of a meal and then, if you feel the need, order more after you've finished. If your favorite entrée is loaded with fat and calories, ask for a half order instead of a full one. Half an order of eggs Benedict may be plenty to satisfy your appetite, but if you have a full order in front of you, you may not have the willpower to quit eating. If the restaurant won't serve a half order, ask the waiter to wrap half before serving it.

In the long run, sensible eating is not about deprivation. If your friends want to take you out for a birthday lunch at the best Sunday buffet spot in town, why not? Splurging once in a while isn't going to hurt.

▮ How to Make a Hearty Breakfast Healthier

If you've always enjoyed a big breakfast, don't stop now. Eating more of your daily calories in the morning is the right idea if you want high energy that lasts through the day and time to burn off calories before bed. Though it isn't always practical to eat your largest meal in the morning, spa nutritionists would agree that eating a big breakfast is fine as long as you eat smaller meals at lunch and dinner and find

some ways to cut the fat and sugar from your hearty breakfast.

When cooking breakfast for yourself or your family, simple substitutions like these suggested by Canyon Ranch in Tucson can make all the difference:

▮ *Use low-fat cream cheese instead of regular cream cheese.*

▮ *Substitute Canadian bacon for regular bacon. It has about one-third fewer calories and one-quarter of the fat.*

▮ *Use 1 percent or even skim milk in your coffee instead of cream. Do the same in recipes for pancakes and waffles.*

▮ *Use only all-fruit jams, jellies and preserves or dried or fresh fruit in place of sugar as a sweetener on toast, pancakes or even cereal.*

▮ *Substitute fructose for sugar in recipes. Fructose is twice as sweet, so you need only half the amount.*

▮ *Vanilla is another good sweetener substitute. Use double the amount stated in a recipe and reduce the sugar by half.*

▮ *Frozen juice concentrates are a good sugar replacement in recipes and also add moisture and flavor. Applesauce is another good option.*

▮ *Use egg whites or egg substitutes instead of whole eggs in recipes, or use only one whole egg and two whites in omelettes.*

▮ *Use water, yogurt or juice in place of oil.*

Spas often serve traditional breakfast dishes with low-fat and low-calorie twists. Even at home, you'll never have to forgo your favorite foods if you follow these calorie-saving recipes.

BLUEBERRY BREAKFAST CAKE

from Canyon Ranch

3 tablespoons margarine, softened

$2/3$ cup fructose

4 egg whites, lightly beaten

1 cup skim milk

1 cup unsweetened applesauce

2 teaspoons vanilla extract

2 cups all-purpose flour

2 cups whole-wheat flour

5 teaspoons baking powder

$1/2$ teaspoon salt

3 cups frozen blueberries

TOPPING

6 tablespoons fructose

$1/2$ cup whole-wheat flour

1 teaspoon cinnamon

2 tablespoons margarine

1. Spray a 10-inch Bundt or tube pan with nonstick cooking spray. Preheat oven to 350°F.

2. Thoroughly cream margarine and fructose in bowl using electric mixer. Add egg whites, milk, applesauce, and vanilla and blend well.

3. In a separate bowl, combine flours, baking powder, and salt. Add to milk mixture and stir until dry ingredients are slightly moistened. Do not overmix.

4. Pour half of batter into prepared pan. Add half of berries, then remaining batter. Top with remaining berries.

5. To make topping, combine fructose, flour, and cinnamon in small bowl. Cut in margarine until crumbly and sprinkle evenly over berries.

6. Bake for 60 to 90 minutes, or until a toothpick inserted near the center comes out dry. Cool in the pan. Unmold onto plate. Turn topping-side up to serve.

Makes 10 to 15 servings

AUTHORS' NOTE: This delicious cake is almost like a bread and can be very filling.

HOMESTYLE POTATOES

from the Cooper Aerobics Center

5 cups unpeeled new potatoes, cooked and diced

$1^1/2$ tablespoons olive oil

$1^1/2$ tablespoons water

$3/4$ teaspoon paprika

$1/2$ teaspoon garlic powder

$1/2$ teaspoon ground black pepper

Dash of cayenne pepper

Pinch of salt

Sprinkle of grated Parmesan cheese

1. Spray a cookie sheet with a nonstick cooking spray. Preheat oven to 425°F.

2. Mix potatoes with oil, water, paprika, garlic powder, peppers, and salt. (Hands work best for mixing.)

3. Spread potato mixture on cookie sheet and bake until crispy, approximately 30 minutes.

4. Sprinkle lightly with Parmesan cheese.

Makes 6 to 8 servings

BREAKFAST SAUSAGE PATTIES

from the Cooper Aerobics Center

1 pound ground turkey breast

³/₄ teaspoon salt

¹/₂ teaspoon ground black pepper

¹/₄ teaspoon dried sage

2 pinches ground nutmeg

2 pinches ground cloves

1 pinch dried oregano

¹/₄ teaspoon garlic powder

1. Mix together all ingredients.

2. Spray a skillet with nonstick cooking spray and warm over medium heat.

3. Form mixture into 12 patties.

4. Place as many patties as possible in skillet and cook until done. Continue until all patties are cooked.

5. Adjust seasoning to taste.

Makes 12 medium-sized patties

BASIC BREAD

from Green Valley Spa and Tennis Resort

2¹/₂ cups water

¹/₃ cup unsweetened apple juice concentrate

1 cup unsweetened applesauce

8 cups whole-wheat flour

1¹/₂ tablespoons active dry yeast

1. Warm water, apple juice, and applesauce in saucepan.

2. Pour in mixing bowl of standing mixer with dough hook in place.

3. Add several cups of whole-wheat flour and mix.

4. Briefly knead on low speed.

5. Add yeast and mix briefly.

6. Knead on low speed while slowly adding additional flour, until dough pulls away from side of bowl. This will normally require most of the flour. (It's better to add too little than too much.) Allow mixer to knead dough until gluten develops, about 10 minutes.

7. With water on hands, remove dough. It should be elastic, with a silky appearance, and should not stick to bowl.

8. Shape into loaves and place in nonstick pans. Let rise in a warm place until doubled in size.

9. Preheat oven to 350°F. Bake for 30 to 45 minutes, depending on size of loaves.

10. Immediately remove from pans and cool on wire rack.

Makes 3 loaves

YOGURT FIG SQUARES

from Lake Austin Spa Resort

2 eggs

2 egg whites

1¹/₂ cups sugar

1 tablespoon vegetable oil

8 ounces baby food prunes

2 cups all-purpose flour

1 teaspoon ground nutmeg

1 teaspoon allspice

1 teaspoon cinnamon

1 teaspoon salt

2 teaspoons baking soda

1 teaspoon baking powder

1 teaspoon vanilla extract

²/₃ cup nonfat plain yogurt

1¹/₂ cups chopped preserved figs

¹/₃ cup pecans, chopped (optional)

1. Preheat oven to 350°F.

2. Beat eggs and whites together. Add sugar, oil, and prunes. Puree.

3. Sift dry ingredients together. Add vanilla to yogurt. Mix dry ingredients with half the egg mixture, then half the yogurt mixture. Mix in remaining egg mixture, then yogurt mixture.

4. Fold in figs and pecans.

5. Spray baking pan with nonstick cooking spray. Pour mixture into pan. Bake for 35 to 40 minutes.

6. Cool.

Makes 12 servings

AUTHORS' NOTE: This cakelike breakfast treat could also be served as a dessert. It is delicious with lemon curd or low-fat whipped cream on top.

APPLE BUTTER

from Miraval Life in Balance

3 pounds Granny Smith apples

2 teaspoons grated fresh ginger

1 tablespoon fresh mint, finely chopped

1 tablespoon orange zest

1 tablespoon lemon zest

¹/₄ cup orange juice

2 tablespoons lemon juice

1 cup honey

³/₄ teaspoon allspice

³/₄ teaspoon cinnamon

1 vanilla bean, split

1 cup golden raisins

1. Peel, core, and chop apples. Combine with remaining ingredients except raisins.

2. In a nonreactive saucepot, bring mixture to a boil, stirring continuously to avoid burning. Reduce heat and simmer, uncovered, stirring occasionally to prevent scorching. Simmer for 45 minutes, until all moisture is evaporated.

3. Remove vanilla bean. Puree mixture and stir in raisins. Allow to cool. Cover and refrigerate.

Makes 2 cups

AUTHORS' NOTE: This butter has the consistency of applesauce. It is great served with chicken, fish or meat, as well as with breakfast foods.

Fast Solutions for Frantic Mornings

If your mornings are so frantic that sitting down for breakfast with your family or by yourself is impossible, you certainly aren't alone. Many families scramble in the morning, but that doesn't mean you should skip breakfast completely. Spas have plenty of solutions for those who need to eat on the run.

A great way to ensure you get the breakfast you need is to pack a bag to go. By brown-bagging foods and saving them for whenever you get a window of free time, such as in your car or at your desk, you'll avoid the temptation to grab a high-fat sweet roll at a fast-food restaurant or off the coffee cart at work. If possible, save your bagged breakfast until you can get away to a favorite outdoor spot for a few moments of peace and quiet.

It helps to fill your refrigerator or pantry

Quick and Easy Smoothies

Spas regularly offer fruit smoothies as a mid-morning or mid-afternoon energy booster. Smoothies also work well for people who need to split their breakfast into two parts. In either case, a smoothie can give you a substantial dose of your day's nutrients and fiber at one sitting. To make a simple smoothie, just blend a banana with yogurt and fruit juice. Spa chefs like to experiment with different fruit combinations and sometimes add nutrient-dense soy or rice milk for variation. You, too, can get as elaborate as your time and imagination allow. By being creative, you, too, can come up with a morning drink suited to your particular taste that will give you as much energy as a three-course breakfast. Use these spa versions to get inspired.

CANTALOUPE YOGURT SHAKE

from Skylonda Fitness Retreat

1/2 medium cantaloupe, diced

1 orange, peeled

2 cups orange juice

1 cup low-fat plain yogurt

2 tablespoons honey

Mix all ingredients in a blender for 2 minutes, or until smooth.

Makes 3 cups

STRAWBERRY SMOOTHIE

from PGA National Resort and Spa

1 1/2 cups strawberries, hulled and halved

2 ripe medium bananas, peeled, frozen, and cut into pieces

8 ice cubes

1/2 cup nonfat vanilla yogurt

1 tablespoon honey

Combine all ingredients in a blender and blend until smooth.

Makes 2 cups

with foods you can grab quickly and eat with one hand and that require no morning preparation. Try whole pieces of fruit, a slice of bread, chunks of low-fat cheese, hard-boiled eggs or low-fat granola eaten dry like trail mix. Better yet, use your weekends to make food like muffins or breads and refrigerate or freeze them for the week ahead. When morning comes you have breakfast waiting.

Low-fat granola and cheese, fruit and well-wrapped breads and bagels all pack well and can go long distances without spoiling. Chefs at spas that specialize in hiking have become very adept at packing breakfast for hikers on the go. There's no reason trail breakfasts can't be as flavorful and interesting as those eaten at home. When you have time to prepare in advance, try one of these delicious breakfast treats made by spas to be enjoyed along the trail.

ILLINI MUFFINS

from the ISPA Collaboration

1 cup blue cornmeal

1 cup all-purpose flour

2 teaspoons baking powder

1/2 teaspoon salt

1/2 cup skim milk

1/2 cup unsweetened applesauce

3 egg whites

1/4 cup honey

1/2 cup orange marmalade

1. Preheat oven to 400°F. Grease 12 muffin cups or line with paper muffin cups.

2. In a large bowl, stir together cornmeal, flour, baking powder, and salt.

3. In another bowl, stir together milk, applesauce, egg whites, and honey. Add to flour mixture all at once, stirring just until dry ingredients are moistened.

4. Spoon 2 tablespoons batter in prepared muffin cups. Top each with 1 teaspoon orange marmalade, then another 2 tablespoons batter. Bake for 25 to 30 minutes, or until muffins are lightly browned.

Makes 12 muffins

PEAR CRISP

from Canyon Ranch

2 cups peeled and thinly sliced pears

(about 1 1/2 ripe pears)

2 1/2 tablespoons all-purpose flour

3 tablespoons thawed apple juice concentrate

3/4 teaspoon cinnamon

Dash ground nutmeg

6 tablespoons graham cracker crumbs

1 1/2 tablespoons melted margarine

1. Preheat oven to 375°F.

2. In an 8-inch square pan, toss pears and 2 tablespoons flour. Add apple juice concentrate and toss to coat pears well.

3. In a bowl, combine remaining flour, spices, and crumbs. Gradually stir in margarine, mixing until the mixture resembles coarse crumbs. Sprinkle evenly over fruit.

4. Bake for 30 minutes, or until topping is lightly browned.

Makes 8 servings

NOTE: You can substitute a 15- to 16-ounce can of water-packed canned pears for fresh pears. Drain them before slicing.

BANANA BRAN MUFFINS

from Rancho La Puerta

1 1/2 cups unprocessed bran*

1/2 cup apple juice

1 egg

3 tablespoons canola oil

1/3 cup honey

1/4 cup buttermilk

1 1/3 cups whole-wheat flour

1 1/4 teaspoons baking soda, sifted

1/4 teaspoon salt

1/2 teaspoon cinnamon

1/4 teaspoon ground cloves

1 ripe banana, peeled and diced, or 3/4 cup fresh or

unthawed frozen blueberries

available at health food stores

1. Preheat oven to 350°F. Line 14 to 16 muffin pan cups (2 1/2-inch diameter) with paper muffin cups.

2. In a medium bowl, combine bran and apple juice. Let sit for 8 minutes.

3. In a large bowl, whisk together egg, oil, honey, and buttermilk.

4. In another medium bowl, combine flour, baking soda, salt, and spices with fork.

5. Combine flour and bran mixtures with liquid mixture and stir just enough to moisten.

6. Fold in bananas until just combined. Do not overmix.

7. Using a ¼-cup dry measure, scoop mixture into muffin cups. (They will be about ⅔ full).

8. Bake for 20 to 25 minutes, or until muffins spring back when pressed.

9. Remove muffins from tins. Cool completely on rack.

Makes 14 to 16 muffins

NOTE: Muffins can be frozen. To serve, defrost, then reheat by placing in foil and baking for 15 to 20 minutes at 350°F.

OLD-TIME GRANOLA

from Rancho La Puerta

2 cups old-fashioned rolled oats

¼ cup raw almonds or hazelnuts, chopped

¼ cup raw sunflower seeds

¼ cup raw wheat germ*

2 tablespoons whole-wheat flour

3 tablespoons wild sage honey*

1 tablespoon cold-pressed safflower oil

½ cup apple juice

½ teaspoon orange zest

2 teaspoons vanilla extract

1 teaspoon cinnamon

½ teaspoon ground coriander

¼ teaspoon ground nutmeg

available at health food stores

1. Preheat oven to 250°F.

2. In a large bowl, toss together all ingredients until well mixed.

3. Spread in thin layer on baking sheet.

4. Bake, stirring often (for even browning), until light brown, 20 to 25 minutes.

5. Let cool on sheet. Transfer to covered container.

Makes 2 cups

NOTE: Granola keeps at room temperature for about 2 weeks.

Reality Check

Recognize the Roadblocks

To start down the path toward a more balanced life, begin by learning what stands in your way. Why aren't you eating a healthful breakfast each morning? Is it because you don't have the time? Or is it because you lack an appetite in the morning or don't care much for typical breakfast food? Once you've identified why you aren't doing something you know will make a difference in your health, you're halfway to finding a workable solution.

BODY WORK

The morning walk is over and you've just finished breakfast. You may feel as though you've already done more for your health than in a full day at home. But at spas the day is still just beginning. The hours between breakfast and lunch are prime exercise time; until you plunge in, you may never know how much you can do or how much you will enjoy it. From step classes to swim clinics, hiking to yoga, weight lifting to line dancing, the exercise options at a spa are vast and eclectic. At some spas, your schedule will be set out for you after a one-on-one consultation. At others, you'll be handed a list of choices so you can plan a schedule yourself. Either way, you have more exercise options, equipment and instruction than you'll ever have at home. Being at a spa provides a great opportunity to find out what it's like to keep your body in motion for two, three, even four hours at a stretch. By the end of the morning, you feel wonderfully spent but also refreshed and very ready for lunch.

Though there may be some lingering notion of spas as "fat farms" promoting crash weight loss programs, nothing could be further from the truth. At today's spas, you'll get the message that staying fit is a lifelong commitment, and you'll go home knowing how to incorporate exercise into your life on an ongoing basis. Although many people actually do lose some weight during their stay at a spa, it's much more important for you to go home knowing how exercising will help take pounds off gradually and keep them off forever.

Weight control is unquestionably one of the key reasons that exercise is so vital to longevity.

But there are immediate, day-to-day rewards from exercise as well. You will begin to look better, stand straighter, sleep more deeply, feel less stressed and have more energy overall. Exercise gives you the opportunity to get back in touch with your body, release tension and renew creativity, and a vigorous workout leaves you calm and energized at the same time, an effect that is hard to achieve any other way. As you become aware of these beneficial side effects of exercise (including some you may never have considered), you may soon change your view of its role in your life. No matter what your age or starting condition, after discovering even a few of the pleasures that come from exercising regularly, you are much more likely to make it a priority in your life.

> ## "Reward yourself for the effort, not the results."
> Julie Waltz Kemble, education director,
> Health and Healing Center, Canyon Ranch

As with your work, loving what you do is a good way to ensure that you stick with an exercise program. At a spa, you'll be introduced to as many fitness options as possible in hopes that you will be excited enough by some to continue them at home. If you've always believed that love and exercise can't exist together, suspend judgment and play the field a bit.

Start by looking around. Find out what's accessible to you indoors, in gyms and classes, and outdoors in whatever part of the country you live in. As you try different activities, spend some time thinking about how various workouts

make you feel as you're doing them and afterward. See if you can pinpoint specific reasons you like or don't like them. Do you need the incentive of working out in a group, or do you prefer reflective solitude? Do you like fast, aggressive exercise such as running, step classes or aerobic dance, in which you really break a sweat, or more focused disciplines, such as t'ai chi or yoga? Are you bored or intimidated? If so, why? There are no right or wrong answers. You're just trying to find out why you like or dislike a type of exercise to help make the process of selection easier.

You may surprise yourself. At the country line-dance class at Canyon Ranch in Tucson, for example, many guests discover that they have a terrific sense of rhythm and want to start dancing at home on Saturday nights. Gaining some skill may be all it takes. That's why the Golden Door in Escondido, Califor-

nia, offers in-line skating for beginners. At home, a lesson can help you overcome the fear that may be holding you back from trying something new. There are plenty of trainers, clinics and classes in all parts of the country where you can turn for help.

Outdoor exercise can be especially motivating. Particularly at spas located in spectacular natural settings, many people are able to put exercise and nature together for the first time and discover a whole new dimension to being physical. The combination of sun, air, scenery and exercise even may inspire you to try something new. Mountain biking in the foothills of Tucson at Miraval Life in Balance, sculling and canoeing at Lake Austin Spa Resort in Austin, Texas, and water workouts in the ocean lagoon at Ihilani Resort and Spa on Oahu, Hawaii, are all ways spas use their natural environments to full advantage.

This is especially true of hiking, the outdoor activity most closely linked with spas. Hiking gives visitors a chance to explore the desert around Canyon Ranch, Miraval Life in Balance and Green Valley Spa and Tennis Resort in St. George, Utah, the redwoods near Skylonda Fitness Resort in Woodside, California, and the mountains around Rancho La Puerta in Baja, California.

If you live in a metropolitan area, you still should be able to find a place to get outside. All cities have parks. You may have to drive some distance to go hiking, but you can certainly find some scenic walks or bike paths even if you live in the heart of a city. Simply getting outside may be enough to give you the day-to-day attitude adjustment you need. In fact, the exercise you choose may soon become secondary to the need to get out in nature on a regular basis.

While you're learning about new activities at a spa, you'll also be learning about the different components of an exercise program and how to balance them. Ideally, a well-rounded exercise program will include aerobic activity like step classes, cycling or hiking, to strengthen the heart, build lung power and burn calories; resistance work, like weight lifting, to prevent loss of muscle and to maintain tone; flexibility exercise, like stretch classes or yoga, to improve ease of motion; and anything—from hiking to dancing—that will put your body through new movement patterns to sharpen your coordination and balance. To achieve overall fitness, you'll need to find a combination of activities that incorporate all of these fundamentals.

The problem, of course, is finding time. One of the significant advantages of a spa visit is the absence of a normal timetable. At a spa, you can take as much time as you need. At home, it can be tough enough to squeeze half an hour of aerobics into a busy day without adding a yoga class or a weight-lifting session on top of it. Let's face it, you don't need an exercise program that actually adds stress by taking up hours you don't have.

Nevertheless, you are going to have to dedicate some time to even an elementary exercise program. If it means getting up a little earlier, sacrificing a leisurely lunch or giving up an hour of television at night, do it. Spas schedule workouts right after breakfast, when energy and motivation are high, but at home, the time to exercise is the time that works best for you, period. Make the time sacred, time you dedicate to yourself no matter what. Absolutely refuse to give it up for anything short of a real emergency. It should be part of your day just like getting to work on time or reading a bedtime story to your children. If you don't save the time to exercise, it will never become an integral part of your life.

Once you've made the commitment, begin by getting your body in motion. That means concentrating on an aerobic activity first and working in strength and flexibility training

later. Even if your schedule or fitness level allows for no more than a fifteen-minute walk once a day, aim to do it five days a week. After you're used to setting aside the time, you can begin increasing the amount of it you spend. In addition, you can slot different activities into the time you've allotted—fast walking one day, yoga the next, for example. Alternating activities serves several purposes. You get all the elements you need into your program, you

> **"Our bodies crave the relaxation that follows hard, physical exertion."**
> Sylvia Sepielli, owner, Sylvia Resorts and Spas

don't get bored and you give your muscles a chance to rest. Adopt activities that can be done inside or out, and learn to adapt to the season and changes in your schedule. Soon, you'll begin to understand how activities blend fitness fundamentals to give you an overall workout in a minimal amount of time. Spa favorites such as hiking, yoga, circuit training, water workouts and dancing can be real time-savers because they combine aerobics, flexibility work, strength building and coordination in various ways.

No matter what you do, start slowly. At a spa, you'll never hear the phrase "no pain, no gain." Aim for long-term results instead of fast ones. Aside from typical muscle soreness, which should serve as assurance that you are working, you should not feel unduly stiff, achy or tired. Especially if you have not exercised in years, it's easy to overestimate how much you can do and to underestimate the amount of rest you need. It's not uncommon for beginners to get through a workout with relative

ease only to find that they can't walk the next day. It's not the performance that reveals your fitness level but how you recover from it. It may be fine to push yourself at a spa, because you'll also be given the time to rest and plenty of muscle-relieving massage, but at home this balancing act is up to you.

If anything, underestimate how much you can do in the beginning. Remind yourself that rest is just as important as exercise in developing fitness. If you take time to listen to what your body is telling you on a daily basis, you should soon discover its natural resilience and capacity for renewal. Keeping a fitness journal is one way to help yourself establish connections between what you do and how you're feeling so that you can make strides more quickly.

Sometimes the easiest way to get started and learn to pace yourself is to place yourself in others' hands. Especially if exercise has been a stumbling block for you in the past, have someone else set up your program. At spas, you'll receive a take-home fitness program to make sure you have the information you need to continue exercising. If you can't get to a spa, it's not difficult to find an expert to help you design an individualized workout program that suits your particular fitness level and needs and that can be worked into your daily schedule. Fitness experts are trained to deflect the most valid anti-exercise excuses and will find ways to help you make exercising part of your day. You don't have to spend the rest of your life in expensive one-on-one sessions. Your goal is to create a program you can work with and to learn the basic skills you need to implement it. You can always go back to the expert to fine-tune or update your workouts.

Classes can be equally beneficial for learning the foundations of exercise. They can introduce you to such basics as body awareness, proper alignment, good breathing and effective heart-rate levels. Teachers are usually happy to answer individual questions. In addition, videos, books and magazine articles are available by the dozens that can tell you which exercises are best for achieving particular results.

Becoming fit can seem complicated, especially when you are trying to achieve an ideal balance of activities. Just remember, exercise doesn't have to be all or nothing. What's important for health, longevity and body maintenance is consistency over time. Do *something*, that's all, and make sure it's something you enjoy. Keep looking for new approaches and challenges to keep your interest level high and your motivation strong. When you are able to stop thinking of exercise as work and start thinking of it as pleasure, it will become exactly what you want it to be: a natural way to get rid of daily stress and revitalize your spirit.

Fundamentals of Fitness

Consider the ways you use your body each day. Stooping to pick up the dog's bowl, climbing stairs, lugging children or shoulder bags or reaching for an item on a high shelf—motions you take for granted—all require a certain level of fitness. Even sedentary activities like typing or driving require muscle strength, coordination, flexibility and at least a minimal amount of cardiovascular endurance.

Fitness is crucial to your ability to function in daily life, and it becomes even more important as you age. Fitness helps to slow the aging process and keeps your body moving in ways that feel easy and natural.

The goal of exercise isn't just to look better or hone your sporting skills. While your abdomen may get flatter and your tennis score may improve as you grow more fit, the most important message about exercise coming

from spas today is that it is essential for feeling and functioning your best, however long you may live. Exercising regularly is one of the best investments in your health and well-being that you can ever make.

To get a good start, you need to know the fundamentals of fitness. Just as good nutrition involves a variety of food groups, overall fitness requires four basic capacities: cardiovascular endurance, strength, flexibility and coordination. Each plays an important role in promoting overall good health and looks and in warding off debilitating stress. While becoming fit may sound like a lot of work, it doesn't have to be. You can focus on different fundamentals on different days or find sports and activities that combine them.

An Aerobic Foundation

The foundation of every fitness program is aerobic exercise—whole-body, rhythmic movement that strengthens the cardiovascular system and builds stamina while burning calories. Even if you never plan to run marathons, take bike trips or play team sports, having a fit heart and lungs will make the physical effort of every single thing you do throughout the day less fatiguing.

Bear in mind that the activity you choose doesn't have to be extreme to be effective. No one, least of all the experts at spas, advocates suffering. Anything you do to get your body moving counts. If you only have time to stroll in the park with your kids, do it. Although it isn't ideal, it's a beginning and valuable to your health. Achieving a more drastic improvement in your fitness level—enough to make you feel stronger, toned and

more energetic—will take more effort. At a minimum, you'll need to elevate your heart rate by doing aerobic exercise for at least twenty minutes three times a week. Though workouts can certainly be vigorous, the effort doesn't have to leave you red-faced and breathless. In fact, it shouldn't.

There's another equally important benefit of aerobic exercise: It helps you deal with the inevitable stress of contemporary life. A vigorous aerobic workout is a great way to release accumulated physical and emotional tension and improve your overall mood. Having a strong cardiovascular system helps your body deal more efficiently with the physical manifestations of stress by "training" your body to handle onslaughts of pressure. Also, the rhythmic quality of aerobic exercise can have a lulling, calming effect after a rough day. Even taking time for a walk in the park or an after-work swim can help you step away from life's pressures for a while and gain some perspective.

Resistance Training for Strength

Strength, or resistance, training, which includes weight lifting and body toning, also has a variety of real-life payoffs. Having defined muscles or a firm body is unquestionably an ego boost. But strengthening your muscles provides benefits that go beyond pride in your appearance. With aging and sedentary living, muscle simply shrinks away unless it receives regular strengthening. Consistent toning workouts can reverse this tendency, improve your posture and help protect against strain, injury and fatigue.

At a minimum, you need to do some basic exercises to strengthen the core of your body—your abdomen and back. So much of your power comes from this central part of your body that shoring up these muscles has far-reaching effects, from enabling you to sit for long hours to improving your ability in almost any sport. Strengthening your core is also essential for preventing and easing back pain.

Having strong legs makes your body better able to support your weight and so takes stress off the back and shoulders. Women, who typically have weaker upper bodies than men, will find that strengthening their arms, shoulders and back will make carrying bags and hoisting children much easier. The benefits don't stop there, either. Every single part of your body, from your toes to your fingers, is connected by muscles. The stronger you make yourself overall, the less tiring daily activities will be.

Resistance or strength training will also enable you to eat more and not gain weight because added muscle burns more calories, even when you're at rest. Finally, strong body muscles, like a strong heart, work as stress barriers, enabling your body to better handle the build-up of tension.

Most people will begin to see benefits from strength training after only a month or two. Weight training even twice a week will tone muscles and help maintain strength, though three workouts a week, or some kind of strength training every other day, is the optimal amount for those who want to achieve major gains. As with aerobics, strength training doesn't have to take hours. As little as twenty minutes of lifting or toning exercises is all you need at one session. A word of caution: If you want to lift weights, it's a good idea to have an expert set up a program designed for your specific ability and needs. Learning proper technique, posture and form is important in order to prevent injuries and achieve the best results.

Flexibility Maintains Ease of Motion

Like strength, flexibility is a requirement for daily life, whether you're bending over to pick up a piece of paper on the floor or working in a garden. It's important to stretch muscles at the end of every aerobic and strength workout, when they are warm and pliable, but you can also stretch throughout the day to maintain ease of motion. Take a break from the computer and do a few stretches for your shoulders and arms. A few minutes of stretching can be so refreshing. Or do some back and leg stretches while watching television at night to help release the tensions built up over the day. Small

breaks like these over the course of a day have more impact than you might imagine. At the very least, you are saying to yourself, "Time out for my body."

As with any fitness activity, those who find stretching easy are likely to find it more of a stress reducer than those who consider it a form of torture and have to be coaxed. There's no question that some people are more naturally flexible than others. Women, in general, tend to be more flexible than men. Yet no matter how stiff you may be when you start, you should begin seeing and feeling results almost immediately. By stretching regularly or doing activities such as yoga or ballet that improve flexibility, you can improve posture and breathing and ease backache and general stiffness. As you improve your muscle elasticity and agility, you'll discover that stretching is a real fountain of youth.

Coordination Pulls It All Together

Last on the list of fitness fundamentals are coordination and balance, often overlooked because they are intrinsic to almost everything physical. They are important not only for athletic skill, but also for building confidence as you move through life. If you've ever successfully negotiated an icy sidewalk or caught yourself before falling, you know how important balance can be. Everything from riding a bicycle to climbing over rocks requires some degree of coordination. As you become more skilled at any sport or exercise, your coordination will improve naturally and you will be able to try more complicated activities.

Best Workouts for Balanced Fitness

The chart below, adapted from one given to guests at Rancho La Puerta, illustrates how activities can be combined to incorporate all the fundamentals of fitness. Use the chart to fine-tune your existing workout regimen or as an inspiration to try something new. Listed are typical activities you can do on your own or offered at local gyms. To save time and make your workouts more interesting, pick activities that combine two, three or even four fundamentals at the same time, such as yoga, water workouts, circuit training, cross-country skiing and hiking. In thirty minutes to an hour, you can get a terrific all-around workout.

	AEROBIC (Cardiovascular)	RESISTANCE (Strength)	FLEXIBILITY	COORDINATION/BALANCE
Walking	■			
Running	■			■
Hiking	■	■		■
Cross-country skiing	■	■		■
Aerobic dance	■			■
Low-Impact aerobics	■			■
Box aerobics	■	■		■
Bicycling	■	■		■
Stationary bike	■			
Swimming	■	■	■	■
Tennis	■			■
Stair climbing	■	■		
Slide	■	■		■
Step	■	■		■
Jumping rope	■			■
Basketball	■			■
In-line skating	■	■		■
Volleyball	■			■
Circuit training	■	■		
Ballet		■	■	■
Ballroom dancing	■			■
Dance fundamentals	■		■	■
Body conditioning		■	■	
Free-weight lifting		■		
Weight machines		■		
Dynabands		■		
Water workouts	■	■	■	■
Hydrofit	■	■	■	■
Stretch 'n tone		■	■	
Pilates™		■	■	
Fit ball		■	■	■
Ab workouts		■		
Ab, bun, thigh workouts		■		
Yoga		■	■	■
Stretching			■	
Back basics		■	■	
T'ai chi			■	■
Sculling/Rowing	■	■	■	■
Rock climbing		■	■	■

Workouts for Weight Loss

Whether or not you lose weight during a visit to a spa, you'll come away understanding that the most important ingredient of a weight loss or maintenance program is, without a doubt, exercise.

At a spa, a typically vigorous workout schedule makes it possible to eat three full meals and still lose weight. But even though you probably can't put in these hours on a home program, you'll still see that the regular exercise you do at home makes it much easier to hold weight gain at bay. You'll be able to eat more—even have that piece of cake or glass of wine—and not gain weight in the long run. Without altering your calorie intake, even moderate amounts of exercise can mean the difference between holding steady and gaining weight. Additionally, eating enough healthful food to meet your body's basic needs combined with regular exercise is the best possible prescription for boosting energy overall. For all these reasons, spa goers who want to lose weight and keep it off are told that the single most important change they can make when they get home is to add exercise to their life.

Even for those with a lot of weight to lose, most spas won't recommend a diet of less than 1,200 calories a day. Instead, they suggest increasing aerobic exercise to burn more calories. Add weight training to your plan and the benefits increase even more. The more muscle you have, the more calories you burn.

A simple formula for losing weight through exercise is based on the calculation that 3,500 calories make up a pound. You can lose half a pound a week without cutting calories by burning off an extra 250 calories a day—approximately an hour of walking or half an hour of jogging or cycling. The number of calories you burn exercising will vary depending on your metabolism, the activity you do, the intensity level and the length of time you exercise. You will have to experiment a bit to discover exactly which combination works best for you. Eventually you should find the balance of food and fitness that helps you maintain a desirable weight and gives you optimal energy at the same time.

The Great Outdoor Gym

One of the overwhelming attractions of many spas is the beautiful outdoor environment they offer for exercise. At home, wherever you live, in the heart of a city or in rural farm country,

Heart Rate Made Simple

Staying within your target heart-rate range is the best way to get an effective aerobic workout. You'll be able to exercise longer, burn more fat and finish feeling refreshed rather than exhausted. While many spas post a target heart-rate chart to help guests determine if they're working out in the right range, there's an equally effective way to judge without a chart if you're working out at home. Instead of counting your pulse, judge your workouts according to how you *feel*. On a scale of very light to very, very hard exertion, you want to feel like you're working out in the middle—or hard enough to break a sweat, but not so hard that you get breathless, red in the face or quickly depleted. This subjective judgment is referred to as perceived exertion and is actually a better way to improve your body awareness.

For an even easier way to monitor intensity, use the "talk test." If you can't carry on a normal conversation while exercising, you are most likely working too hard. Slow down. If, on the other hand, you can sing normally while exercising, you are probably not working hard enough and need to pick up the pace a bit.

taking a break from the daily grind to get some sunshine and fresh air may do you as much good as the exercise. Those with indoor jobs, in particular, may not find it nearly as motivating to work out inside too. Exercising outdoors makes it easier to spend quality time with your partner, the kids or the dog, or even some time alone with nature. The fresh air will clear your head, and there's even a good chance you will revitalize your outlook on life as you firm up your body.

The biggest challenge for those of you seeking to take advantage of outdoor exercise is finding ways to implement all the fundamentals of fitness so that you get workouts that are as balanced as those you get in a gym. A closer look at your environment, however, will reveal all sorts of possibilities in stairs, curbs, park benches, trees and even rocks. Because you have more space to move outdoors, you actually have more opportunities to be creative, and the more variety you put into your workout, the more you hone the motor skills you'll need to keep primed as you age.

The Golden Door is such a strong advocate of using the great outdoors for exercise that it has developed a class in outdoor cross-training. Aerobic runs, hikes and walks can be cardiovascular workouts and strength, flexibility and coordination sessions at the same time. Use these tips from the Golden Door and other spas as a jumping-off point for creating your own outdoor regimen. If you feel awkward about trying these on a public trail or path, find a track or field where athletes practice.

■ **For upper-body strength:** *Do push-ups against a wall, tree or park bench. Turn around and do dips for your triceps off the edge of a* bench or large rock. Use a jungle gym or sturdy tree branch for pull-ups.

For aerobic power:
▶ After warming up with a fifteen- or twenty-minute walk, add some lung-and-heart-strengthening intervals. Speed up and walk or run as fast as you can for two minutes, then slow down for one minute. Add more intervals to your workout as you get stronger.

▶ Keep your heart rate high on the downhill portion of hikes by adding squats or lunges.

For lower-body toning: Use a curb or stairs for a step workout. Make it tougher by jumping on and off with both feet together. Or climb stairs two steps at a time. Depending on how many stairs you have, you may need to make multiple trips.

For coordination and balance:
▶ Vary your walking techniques. Lift your knees as high as you can, then crouch down and do the shuffle, touching your hands to the ground. Now walk sideways, crossing your legs in a "grapevine" fashion, then practice walking backward. To help strengthen foot and ankle muscles you don't work through regular walking, alternate walking on the outside of your feet, then the inside.

▶ Try walking along a curb without falling off. Then stand on one leg for up to thirty seconds. Switch legs.

▶ On soft ground or padded surfaces, practice broad jumps, springing as high and as far as possible. Or try skipping as high as you can.

▶ Find a line of rocks or set up traffic cones, and, running or walking, weave in and out to help develop timing and coordination.

▌**For flexibility:** *Finish your workout with some stretches: Lean against a park bench for calf stretches. Drop heels off a stair or curb. Use a tree or swing set for arm stretches.*

▌Glorious Hiking

Hiking is often at the heart of the spa experience, and it isn't hard to understand why. It is superb physical exercise that is also gratifying to the mind and spirit. Hiking can clear your mind and give you a fresh perspective. Many individuals who first try hiking at a spa get so hooked they find ways to continue when they get home.

Hiking is universally popular for another reason. It's something anyone can do. Technically speaking, it's another form of walking, so if you can walk, you can hike at some level. Hiking can be anything from a steady-paced stride on flat terrain to scrambling over rocks, up cliffs and along steep passages that challenge your skill. The tougher the hike, the more demand is placed on your cardiovascular system and your legs and hips. Maneuvering over rocks and steep slopes promotes agility and coordination and hones concentration and focus.

> **"On a trail, with the wind in your face, you start seeing nature, hearing nature, and the mind becomes very clear."**
>
> Dixon Collins, founder, Skylonda Fitness Retreat

As you become a more adept hiker, you'll develop confidence and ease with being in nature. You'll discover sights, sounds and scents you won't find in a city and experience a physical thrill that you can never feel on a treadmill, no matter how much you manipulate the speed and incline controls.

At a spa, you won't have to worry about directions or other details that might distract you from the environment. There is always at least one experienced staff member hiking with you, and often two or three, to make sure no one is left behind. These hike leaders are generally in charge of carrying heavy packs, extra water, snacks, first-aid kits and communication devices in case of trouble. It's a bonus if they are well versed in regional history, flora and fauna, and can point out pertinent sights as you go.

Short of hiring your own private sherpa, you won't get the same tender loving care at home. You'll need to make sure you are carrying proper clothing, sunscreen, hats, maps, ample water and food and anything else you will need for the amount of time you plan to be gone. Always let someone know when you are leaving, where you are planning to go and when you plan to return. You must take into account the difficulty of the terrain, the unpredictability of the weather and such potential natural disasters as bee stings, cactus pricks or falls.

It's best to never hike alone, and it helps to have a traveling companion or two who are familiar with the terrain when you hike in a new area. Sometimes the best way to find hiking partners is by joining a local hiking group. To locate one, contact local branches of wilderness organizations or check your local health club for weekend outings. Call your regional or state parks department for information on nearby hiking areas, ranger-led tours and other back country updates.

Hiking can be sublime, but it requires attention to mundane details. You can't immerse yourself in a beautiful environment

without being well prepared with some basic hiking techniques. So you can be more comfortable in the wilderness, even on unfamiliar trails, here are some tips to keep in mind from spas that specialize in hiking—Canyon Ranch, Rancho La Puerta and Skylonda.

▌**Mind your feet.** *Even the best-fitting boots can cause problems on long hikes, so part of becoming an experienced hiker is learning to take foot irritations in stride. Bring blister protection and apply it at the first sign of rubbing or irritation. Better yet, if you have a history of sore spots, protect your feet before you leave.*

▌**Loosen up.** *Before a hike, a short stretch will keep you limber. Stretching after a hike is even*

more important, since it wards off post-hike soreness and muscle stiffness. Pay particular attention to your calves, shins, thighs, hips and shoulders.

▌**Negotiate hills.** *Hill climbing is one of the greatest challenges of hiking and can bring the greatest satisfaction. It helps to know some simple ways to negotiate the ups and downs to minimize stress, strain and anxiety. When going uphill, power yourself by straightening your back leg in a push-off motion. On really tough ascents, take small steps, placing your whole foot on the ground instead of just your toes. Keep your pace steady. On descents, bend your knees. If the slope is steep, turn your feet out and take smaller steps. If the path is slippery, dig in your heels for better traction.*

A Hike in Solitude

It's true that hiking promotes camaraderie, and you may look forward to those friendly conversations on the trail. Yet the moments you spend alone in nature, immersed in the outdoors, are often the times you remember most vividly. Although it isn't a good idea to set out on an entire hike alone, you and a partner can separate for a brief interval of solitude, then meet up again to complete the hike. Even if you start out hiking with a large group, you can choose to split up for a short time and spend some solitary time meditating on the beauty around you. To give it a try, here are some ideas from a hike introduced at Skylonda.

Set off along the trail at two-minute intervals or longer, so as to maintain space between the person in front of and behind you. If you find yourself catching up to the person in front of you, slow down or stop for a minute.

Whoever leads the hike should clearly mark the trail so that everyone knows which way to go. If you decide to do only a portion of your hike in solitude, be sure to pick specific beginning and end points.

If possible, do the portion in solitude in an area of particular beauty, leaving time for quiet reflection after.

Use your time alone to notice the world around you and to discover the unique character of your environment. Pay attention to the sounds, sights, smells, textures and colors. Look closely at the flowers, trees and animals. The world you experience will be different from the one you encounter in a group.

Catch your breath. *Steep hills and long climbs can make even the fittest hiker feel breathless. If you are having trouble catching your breath, first make sure your back is straight and you're not bent forward. To get your breathing even again, try a technique called the "double breath." Blow twice quickly through your mouth, then inhale and repeat if needed.*

You can also try slowing down and pacing your steps to the rhythm of your breath. Take three, two or even one step for each inhale-and-exhale cycle, and concentrate on breathing deeply and evenly. Imagine filling your rib cage from your waist all the way to your collarbone and exhaling just as fully. With better breathing, you'll have more stamina for even vigorous hikes.

Water Workouts: A Low-Impact Alternative

A spa's daily lineup of activities almost always includes classes that take place in a pool. In the days when many spa visitors weren't regular exercisers, pool workouts were something they could do without developing undue muscle soreness. Today they're still in fashion, and beneficial to even the most fit. At some spas, like the Greenhouse in Dallas, aquatic workouts comprise a large part of the daily agenda. From dancelike classes in shallow pools equipped with ballet barres, to deep-water workouts utilizing flotation devices, water workouts are a terrific alternative to high-impact exercise.

Practical reasons aside, getting into the water is fun. For many, it's a return to childhood,

when playing in a pool was a favorite recreational activity. You'll emerge from an hour in the water with those same feelings of exhilaration and relaxation you had as a kid.

Water classes are very beneficial to those who haven't exercised in a long time or who have never exercised. Because of the buoyant quality of the water, you can do all the same moves you would do on land—walking, running, jumping, kicking—without the strain and impact. For those doing land workouts as well, water exercise is a relaxing alternative on days when your body feels particularly stiff or sore. It is also a safe alternative for those with back problems or other injuries.

At the same time, water classes are not just for the out-of-shape and infirm. Just because you don't feel the impact doesn't mean your body isn't working. If you've ever walked through knee-deep water at the beach, with resistance making each step slow and laborious, you already know what a workout you can get in water. And the more of your body that is submerged, the more resistance you create, giving you a better all-around workout.

Deep-water workouts, those in which you are suspended in water, are the most difficult, because every move meets with resistance. If you wear a flotation vest, you can run without ever touching bottom for a very strenuous and impact-free aerobic workout.

You might also try buoyant ankle cuffs, which suspend you in the water while you perform lower-body toning exercises, and Styrofoam dumbbells and webbed gloves, which provide upper-body workouts. Kickboards and plastic dumbbells are other equipment that make water workouts both fun and beneficial.

Despite all the creative devices on the market today, you don't need any equipment to enjoy the water. If you'd like to try something new but don't have access to a water class, you can improvise your own water workout. All you need is a body of water and these simple ideas to get you started:

▪ *Start by walking in water that's knee to chest deep. Since you'll be moving fairly slowly, pay attention to your breathing and heart rate to determine how hard you're working. Especially on sand, roll all the way through your foot from the heel to the toes to strengthen foot and leg muscles.*

▪ *To add all-around leg toning, take fifty steps forward, fifty steps sideways in a "grapevine" motion, fifty steps backward and then fifty steps to the other side.*

▪ *To tone the chest, upper back and shoulder muscles, submerge yourself from the neck down. Start with your arms straight out from your sides. Keeping the elbows slightly bent, pull your palms toward each other in a clapping motion. Then, when your fingers touch, reverse the motion. Turn your palms out and push your arms away from each other and then behind you as far as possible without straining. Reverse and repeat.*

▪ Listen to Your Body

Try this simple exercise. Stand in front of a full-length mirror and focus on your body for three full minutes, never removing your eyes from your reflection. If you're like most people, this won't be easy. After a few seconds, you'll find your eyes moving to other objects reflected in the mirror while your mind follows suit, ready to think about any other subject than what you look like. It's not unusual to be so out of touch with your physical self that you can't even bear to look at your body for more than a few seconds, much less listen to it.

The exercise above is taught at Miraval Life in Balance to help guests begin listening to their bodies. Learning to pay attention to the physical sensations you are experiencing and to be more comfortable simply looking at yourself are the first steps toward real body awareness.

The benefits of developing body awareness are more far-reaching than you might imagine. If you're in tune with what your body is telling you, you'll not only understand how you can best divert stress and achieve greater relaxation, but you may even be able to detect injury and illness at the onset and to get help more quickly. Strictly from a fitness point of view, learning to listen to your body can help you get the most from a workout.

Though you will still get physical benefits when your mind is in a detached state, you're not getting the best workout possible. By practicing mindfulness while you work out, instead of reading a book or watching television to make time pass more quickly, you can turn an exercise session into time devoted entirely to your body. Next time you're on a treadmill, pay

some attention to what's happening physically. Is one leg working harder than the other? Are your hands clenched or relaxed? Are you breathing easily or gasping for air? When you perform an exercise, are the right muscles doing the work? Does your shoulder hurt when you lift weights a certain way? If you ignore that pain now, you are setting yourself up for almost certain injury.

Body mindfulness is one way of getting in touch with the natural unity of your body and mind. You get the best results when the two work together to achieve one purpose. Not only will you better serve your body by listening to its needs, but you'll get a great workout at the same time. Here are some suggestions from Miraval Life in Balance on ways to use body mindfulness in your workout.

▮ *Scan your body as you walk on a treadmill. Begin by concentrating on the balls of your feet. Think about the way they feel as you walk. Then*

shift your attention to your heels, to your calves and so on all the way up to the top of your head. This exercise will help you keep your mind in the present and focused specifically on what your body is doing from moment to moment.

▮ *Breathe through your whole body as you lift weights. Pretend there's a tube running from the top of your head to the bottom of your feet. As you push or lift the weight, exhale quickly, imagining your breath coming from your feet and shooting out the top of your head. As you release the weight, inhale for six counts, imagining the air moving from your head down through your body and into your feet. This exercise helps you develop awareness of your whole body and allows your energy to move freely.*

▮ *Zero in on the muscles actually doing the work. When you first perform an exercise, particularly with weights, do it at a super-slow speed. Notice* the physical sensation as you move. Where do you feel tension? Are the right muscles doing the work? Can you shift the exercise slightly so that they are? Can you let go of tension where you don't need it? If you can begin to isolate areas you want to tone, you'll start to see results much faster.

▎ Stop at least three times during the day and pay attention to what your body is saying. Is it telling you to eat, exercise, rest, or slow down? By noticing how you respond to stress right away, you can keep your responses from getting out of hand.

Keeping Track of Fitness

Keeping a record of your workouts will help you better understand how your body responds to exercise. By logging in items like distance, speed, weather conditions, time of day, how you were feeling at the time, where you might push harder and where you need to ease up, you'll be keeping track of information that can help you reach the fitness level you desire. For example, journal notations over the course of a couple of weeks will easily red-flag such points as when your energy level is at its highest and which exercises irritate old injuries.

A fitness journal can even help reveal how your body responds to exercise. If your heart rate jumps too high whenever you use a stair climber, for instance, but stays within target range on the treadmill, you'll know it in a short period of time. Your journal may help you understand the effect outdoor tempera-

tures have on your ability to exercise. If you keep an exercise journal long term, you will have a guide that can lead you as expertly as any coach or trainer.

As with any journal, there is no right or wrong way to keep one. If you are trying to reach a specific goal or have started a new or complicated activity, such as weight training, you may want to keep a more formal record with lots of specific data that will give you a clear progress report. If you just want to keep track of basics, like time and distance, an informal journal can work fine. However you choose to keep your records, write down observations that seem important to you. Weekly and monthly charts can help you see the big picture.

In any journal, there are a few basics to keep in mind: date, type of exercise, time performed, how you felt and other pertinent comments that will help you know how to make changes in the future.

Reality Check

Consider Your Alternatives

Even the most committed exerciser will have days when plans go awry. The solution is to have lots of alternatives. Be prepared if something gets in the way of your regular workout. If you have to work through your exercise hour, make a promise to exercise later. If you like to work out outdoors, have indoor options when the weather turns bad. When you travel, take walking shoes or a routine you can do anywhere. Make a commitment to get your body moving in some way every day, then adjust to circumstances to keep that commitment.

ENERGY FOR THE AFTERNOON

The morning walk is a fond memory. After breakfast you may have taken two or three consecutive exercise classes. You're probably tired but feeling better than you have in years. Now it's time for lunch, and suddenly you realize you're ravenous. Lunch at a spa is served casually—around the pool, on a patio or buffet-style in the dining room. It's a time to relax with other guests, a chance to get better acquainted with the person you met on the morning walk or in the hot tub. You'll be lunching in a robe, shorts and a T-shirt or leotards and tights. No one notices what you're wearing. The focus is on the food—plentiful, appealing and balanced just right to carry you through the afternoon.

If breakfast sets the tone for your morning, lunch sets the pace for the afternoon. What you eat for your midday meal determines whether you will drag through the rest of the day or stay mentally sharp and motivated. A well-balanced lunch can improve your afternoon performance, helping you to stay focused and attentive, light on your feet and full of energy. What you eat for lunch can even improve your mood.

At spas, the midday meal makes up about one-third of all the food you'll eat in a day. It is substantial and filling but not heavy—an important balance whether you'll be exercising, working or even relaxing in the afternoon. You'll find the same kinds of food you like at home: sandwiches, salads, soups, burgers and pizza. But at spas, these classics are low in fat and light on bread, while favoring lean meat, small amounts of cheese and lots of vegetables—a mix that will keep you going through the busiest afternoon.

Eating starchy carbohydrates such as cereal and toast at breakfast will give you energy and brain power, but too much bread and pasta at lunch may soon have you begging for a siesta. Instead, save starchy foods for dinner, when you are winding down before sleep. For energy at lunch, moderate amounts of lean protein, like fish, chicken or turkey work best.

Eating smaller portions and avoiding fatty foods will also keep you from feeling groggy in the afternoon. That may not always be an easy rule to follow when you are at the mercy of the next-door deli, where the sandwiches can be so huge that just one supplies most of the calories and fat you need in an entire day. Opt instead for smaller versions, or eat half of a

> **"Keep your lunch light. Americans don't get siestas."**
> Cheryl Hartsough, nutritionist, PGA National Resort and Spa

large one. Choose whole-grain bread and avoid fatty luncheon meats, tuna in mayonnaise and piles of cheese. This way, you can put together a sandwich with all the ingredients of a well-balanced meal.

For a good model, take a look at typical spa sandwiches. These include vegetarian and turkey sandwiches on whole-grain bread, sliced chicken in pita pockets, and open-faced grilled fish or vegetable sandwiches that leave you feeling satisfied and replenished instead of overstuffed. For diehard burger-lovers, spas substitute vegetables, beans or turkey for the beef and put the burger on a small whole-wheat bun.

Warm foods tend to fill you up, so sipping soup before lunch can help curb your appetite. A cup of soup makes a great starter, and spas often begin lunch this way. If it's hearty enough, made with lots of vegetables, beans or lean meat, it can become an entire meal. Besides, on a cold day, there is little that is more satisfying than a cup of steaming hot soup sipped slowly by a fire, and when it's hot outside, cold vegetable and fruit soups are cooling and filling at the same time.

Vegetables are of prime importance in any soup, salad or sandwich listed on a spa's lunch menu. Ideally, vegetables should play a major role in your lunch as well, with meat and cheese the supporting players instead of the other way around. Make it a habit to consume a large plate of colorful vegetables with every luncheon entrée. As you add various colors to your plate, you can be assured of getting the full range of vitamins and minerals that vegetables have to offer. At spas, you'll find five or six different vegetables decorating a luncheon plate. Be generous when adding extra vegetables to all your soups and sandwiches. Thin-crust pizza made with lots of vegetables and small amounts of cheese, for example, is a fine option. If you aren't a big vegetable eater already, this is a painless way of introducing them into your diet.

Salads are another excellent vegetable-rich choice for lunch. Add a little chicken, turkey or fish and you have a well-balanced meal. Many spas are known for serving inventive salads with such combinations as chicken and grapes, apples and cabbage and papaya, onion and basil. At home you can make versions of salads that easily compete with those served at spas. Start with the freshest and most nutritious greens available, add lots of colorful vegetables and toss them with a low-fat dressing. Choose one of the many prebottled selections lining grocery store shelves today, or try one of the dressing recipes from spas included in this chapter.

Besides creating innovative salads, spa chefs often come up with their own interpretations of ethnic cuisines using regional vegetables and spices. At the Ihilani Resort and Spa on Oahu, Hawaii, for example, char siu chicken with Chinese long beans and a buckwheat soba salad with Asian vegetables appear frequently on the lunch menu. The Claremont Resort and Spa in Berkeley, California, serves up its own version of Chinese cuisine in a stir-fry, another easy way to mix up vegetables for lunch and a dish prepared creatively at many spas. In the Southwest, spas such as Lake Austin Spa Resort in Austin and the Greenhouse in Dallas offer Mexican-inspired dishes ranging from eggplant enchiladas to low-fat quesadillas. Go ahead and pile on the salsa.

In every city, ethnic restaurants offer great choices for lunch. Japanese broiled fish, rice and vegetables, Indian yogurt-based curry dishes or a Thai soup and salad are tasty, healthful choices. You will need to be savvy about weeding out high-fat items, such as deep-fried vegetables and coconut milk sauces, but overall ethnic restaurants give you a large selection of foods that will see you through the afternoon.

Once you're comfortable making food choices, follow the spa example and make sure lunch becomes a real time-out from work, play or

whatever else you are doing in your day. Instead of grabbing the first food you can find to gobble on the run, see if you can set some time aside to concentrate on your meal and give your mind and body a rest. If a crazy day prevents lunch from being a relaxed event, getting away from whatever you're doing for as little as fifteen or twenty minutes can work wonders. If you're at home, set up a tray or the table with silverware, even if you're all alone. Sit back and savor every bite. *How* you put energy into your body is just as important as *what* you put into it. If you rush through lunch, you won't feel

satisfied when you're done, and nervous eating will just result in nervous energy. Slow down, take stock. Let the afternoon soar.

Fundamentals of Lunch

As with breakfast, spa lunches vary in style, but generally the midday meal includes lots of vegetables and a good amount of the recommended daily servings of protein from meat, fish, poultry, cheese or beans. If you haven't been to

a spa and don't have a good conception of a balanced lunch, the food pyramid—illustrating the government's guidelines for a healthful diet—can be a good tool for guiding you to the kinds and amounts of food you need at lunch to give you optimal energy in the afternoon.

As you can see from the pyramid, vegetables should be a large part of your diet. The guidelines suggest three to five servings of vegetables each day; the exact amount depends on your size, sex and activity level. A single serving is one cup of leafy raw vegetables, one-half cup of chopped raw vegetables or one-half cup of cooked vegetables. By eating vegetables steamed or in salads and soups at lunch, you can meet most of your daily vegetable needs.

Most vegetables are high in fiber, which you need every day. Many, particularly the green, leafy varieties, are extremely low in calories and have virtually no fat. Feel free to eat them in quantity as long as you stay away from high-fat dressings, sauces and toppings. Having hot spinach salad with dressing made from bacon grease, for example, almost cancels out the nutritional benefits of the greens because you are adding so much fat. Instead, try low-fat cottage cheese or yogurt on top of your salad or experiment with flavorful, low-fat dressings.

With the wide array of fresh and organic vegetables now available in supermarkets and greenmarkets, finding ones you like should be easy. Go for variety. Try to include everything from dark green, leafy types like chard, kale and spinach to bright red and yellow tomatoes and peppers, meaty eggplants, potatoes and squash. The richer and deeper the color, the more nutritious the vegetable, and the more colorful the array, the more you can be sure you're getting the most nutritional benefits.

Vegetarian spas rely heavily on beans when creating meals. Beans, another good nutritional addition to any lunch, are one of the best low-fat, low-calorie, high-fiber vegetables available. Beans are included in the meat portion of the pyramid because they are also a good source of protein. Think of them as a crossover vegetable—an alternative to meat or great as a side dish.

Although low-calorie vegetables may be consumed in larger quantities, you will need to pay close attention to the amount of protein you consume at lunch. The pyramid suggests two to three servings of meat, poultry, fish, beans, nuts and eggs in a day, or five to seven ounces total. It's fine to eat your entire daily allotment at lunch if you want, but if you eat a hefty eight-ounce burger or a twelve-ounce steak at one sitting, you actually are getting more protein than you need in an entire day.

To visualize the proper amount, think of one serving as about the same size as a pack of cards. It might help you to use a food scale until you get an idea of the right amount. A few slices of chicken, a small piece of grilled fish or a small turkey burger is all you need. If you add cheese—a fine option at lunch—remember that only 1½ ounces comprises one of the two to three daily servings of dairy products recommended in the federal guidelines. Again, you don't have to follow the pyramid exactly, but it can help you choose a balanced lunch that will serve you well till dinner.

Mood-Altering Foods

Eat too much, you feel sluggish. Eat too little, you can't think straight. A plate of pasta makes you sleepy, a candy bar gives you a quick lift that doesn't last. Food is so intimately tied to your mood that chances are you automatically reach for certain foods when you need a boost. At the Claremont in Berkeley, California, as well as at the PGA National Resort and Spa in Palm Beach Gardens, Florida, guests can discover how to use those impulses to their advantage by learning how healthful foods can be mood enhancers.

Complex carbohydrates at lunch may help calm you when you are anxious, tense or stressed from morning activities, but too much may put you to sleep. You'll need to experiment to find the amount that works best for you. When you are feeling particularly edgy, try adding one of the following to your lunch: three pieces of fresh fruit or a little dried fruit, half a cup of pasta or rice, a slice of whole-grain bread or a small baked potato.

Lean protein will help wake you up and keep you feeling alert when you are sleepy or lethargic. It also works well when you have a long, busy afternoon ahead and need to be "on." For lunch, try a hard-boiled egg or an egg-white omelette, broiled or baked fish or poultry or a little cheese.

Eggs, dairy products and lean protein are all good spirit lifters when you are feeling depressed or a little low. Legumes like beans and nuts may help as well. Try ordering rice and beans or a soy-burger for lunch to give yourself a boost. Other good options are a vegetable stir-fry with tofu (light on the oil) or some low-fat hummus.

Spa-Style Sandwiches

Sandwiches can be real energy-boosters when they're made with lean meats, whole grains and lots of vegetables. To make a sandwich more healthful, start with the bread. Follow the lead of spa chefs and use whole-grain breads or pita pockets. Pay attention to the size of the bread. Cut a baguette into fourths, or, if bread slices are thick, make an open-faced sandwich using only one piece of bread. If your sandwich still looks big enough for two, eat only half the sandwich and save the rest for a snack.

Instead of using mayonnaise or ketchup, flavor your sandwiches with mustard, herbs or a low-fat spread. If you use mayonnaise, put it on only one piece of bread and scrape it on thinly instead of slathering. Substitute grilled fish, lean beef, chicken or turkey for processed luncheon meats and fatty sausages like salami or bratwurst.

If you are partial to thick sandwiches, try using half as much meat and cheese and doubling the amount of vegetables. In fact, add vegetables like tomato, onion, sprouts or cucumber whenever possible. Grilled vegetable sandwiches made with everything from red peppers to yellow squash are so delicious that you may never miss the meat. To achieve the same consistency and thickness as a corned beef or pastrami sandwich, try thick slabs of grilled eggplant topped with tofu and onion.

Burgers also come in many versions other than beef. Turkey burgers, vegetable burgers, bean burgers and fish burgers can be delicious alternatives. Adding garlic and herbs such as basil, rosemary and sage provides more flavor to these burgers than mayonnaise and ketchup. With extra time, you can make your own whole-wheat buns for burgers, too.

Even pizzas lose nothing but calories when made with a thin crust and piles of vegetables and spices instead of heavy cheese and pepperoni. In fact, many spas feature pizza on their lunch menus. To make your own pizza or inventive, healthful sandwiches, try these spa recipes.

EGGPLANT PITA POCKET

from Norwich Inn & Spa

DRESSING

1 tablespoon diced shallots

$1/8$ teaspoon diced garlic

2 teaspoons peeled, seeded, and diced tomato

2 tablespoons safflower oil

3 tablespoons red-wine vinegar

1 teaspoon olive oil

$1/2$ eggplant, diced in $1/4$-inch pieces

1 clove garlic, roasted and minced

3 teaspoons roasted and diced red bell pepper

$1/4$ teaspoon salt

1 dash ground black pepper

4 whole-wheat pita pockets, halved

1 ounce feta cheese

$1/2$ cup radish sprouts

1. To make dressing, combine shallots, garlic, and tomatoes. Whisk together vinegar and safflower oil. Add to tomato and shallot mixture.

2. Preheat oven to 425°F.

3. Spread olive oil evenly on baking sheet. Spread diced eggplant on sheet and roast until tender, about 5 minutes. Remove.

4. Combine eggplant, garlic, bell pepper, and salt and pepper in a bowl. Mix in the dressing and toss. Place a heaping tablespoon of mixture in each pita half. Add sprinkling of cheese and sprouts.

Makes 8 servings

VEGETARIAN BURGER

from the Doral Golf Resort and Spa

1 cup shredded carrots

$3/4$ cup cooked brown rice

$1/3$ cup minced yellow onion

2 tablespoons roasted walnut pieces, finely chopped

$1/4$ cup whole-wheat breadcrumbs

$1/2$ cup mixed shitake and button mushrooms

1 tablespoon chopped parsley

2 egg whites, lightly beaten

1 tablespoon Worcestershire sauce

1 teaspoon Dijon mustard

Splash lite soy sauce

2 whole-wheat pita pockets

4 slices tomato

4 pieces lettuce

1. Preheat oven to 350°F.

2. Mix all ingredients except pita pockets, tomato and lettuce by hand until blended.

3. Chill for 1 to 2 hours.

4. Form into 4 patties (for lighter appetites) or 2 patties (for larger appetites).

5. Coat baking sheet with nonstick cooking spray and place burgers on sheet.

6. Bake for 5 minutes. Turn. Bake an additional 5 minutes, or until both sides are crispy. Place small burgers in pita halves with slice of tomato and piece of lettuce. Place large burgers in whole pitas with two slices tomato and two pieces lettuce.

Makes four 4-ounce burgers or two 8-ounce burgers

TURKEY BURGERS
from the Golden Door

PATTIES

2 pounds ground, skinless turkey breast

2 tablespoons minced shallots

2 tablespoons minced fresh parsley

2 tablespoons minced fresh tarragon

Freshly ground black pepper to taste

1. Preheat a grill.

2. Mix all ingredients by hand.

3. Form into 8 patties, about 3 $\frac{1}{2}$ inches in diameter.

4. On a hot grill, cook patties on both sides until cooked but still juicy, about 8 minutes per side.

Makes 8 patties

GARLIC WHEAT BUNS

1 tablespoon (1 packet) active dry yeast

1 $\frac{1}{4}$ cups tepid water

1 teaspoon honey

1 teaspoon salt

1 teaspoon olive oil

1 tablespoon minced garlic

1 tablespoon minced fresh rosemary

$\frac{1}{2}$ cup whole-wheat flour

2 cups unbleached all-purpose flour, plus additional to dust dough and work surfaces

1. In mixing bowl, combine yeast, water, honey, and salt. Let yeast activate for about 10 minutes.

2. Heat nonstick pan over medium heat. Add olive oil. Add garlic and rosemary and stir with wooden spoon until garlic softens. Set aside to cool.

3. With dough hook or by hand, gradually mix the yeast mixture, whole-wheat flour, all-purpose flour, garlic, and rosemary to make a soft, elastic dough. Knead for 1 to 2 minutes. Gather dough into a ball and sprinkle with flour. Cover and let rise in a warm place until double in bulk.

4. When dough has risen, transfer onto a floured board and knead well with hands. Cut into 8 pieces. With lightly floured hands, roll in palms to make 2 $\frac{1}{2}$-inch to 3-inch rounds. Flatten. Transfer to baking sheet. Let rise for 10 minutes.

5. Preheat oven to 400°F. Bake buns for 25 to 30 minutes, until lightly browned and crusty.

Makes 8 buns

VEGETABLE PIZZA
from Rancho La Puerta

1 recipe Whole-Wheat Pizza Dough (*see page 63*)

1 $\frac{1}{2}$ cups Fresh Tomato-Basil Sauce (*see page 63*)

$\frac{1}{4}$ cup chopped fresh basil or 1 $\frac{1}{2}$ teaspoons dried

3 tablespoons chopped fresh oregano or 1 $\frac{1}{2}$ teaspoons dried

2 tablespoons freshly grated Parmesan cheese

3 small zucchini, cut in $\frac{1}{4}$-inch slices

2 medium green or red bell peppers, cut in thin strips

8 ounces fresh mushrooms, thinly sliced

$\frac{3}{4}$ cup (2 ounces) freshly grated part-skim mozzarella cheese

1. Preheat oven to 425°F.

2. Lightly brush two large baking sheets with vegetable oil.

3. Roll each ball of dough into a 7-inch circle, flouring if dough sticks to work surface. Set rolled dough on baking sheets. Fold over edges of dough $\frac{1}{2}$ inch around and crimp. Set aside to rise for 15 minutes.

4. Spoon ¹/₄ cup Fresh Tomato-Basil Sauce over each pizza. Sprinkle with basil, oregano, and Parmesan cheese. Arrange vegetables over pizzas. Top with mozzarella cheese.

5. Bake for 20 minutes, or until crusts are golden.

Makes 6 pizzas

WHOLE-WHEAT PIZZA DOUGH

³/₄ cup plus 2 tablespoons tepid water

2 teaspoons olive oil

1 teaspoon dried oregano

1 teaspoon dried basil

1 teaspoon minced garlic

2 teaspoons honey

1 tablespoon (1 packet) active dry yeast

1 cup whole-wheat flour

1 cup unbleached all-purpose flour

¹/₄ teaspoon sea salt

1. In small bowl, combine water, oil, herbs, garlic, and honey. Stir in yeast. Let stand until frothy, about 5 minutes.

2. In large bowl, combine flours and salt. Pour yeast mixture over flour and stir until combined.

3. Transfer dough to floured surface. Knead dough until smooth and soft. Shape into a ball. Set in a large bowl that has been lightly brushed with vegetable oil. Turn dough once. Cover bowl. Allow to rise in warm place for about 45 minutes, or until double in volume.

4. Divide into 6 pieces. Knead each ball until smooth.

Makes 6 dough balls

FRESH TOMATO-BASIL SAUCE

3¹/₂ pounds tomatoes, chopped

1 cup chopped onion

5 garlic cloves, minced

6 fresh thyme sprigs or 1 teaspoon dried thyme leaves

1 bay leaf

¹/₄ teaspoon dried chile flakes

1 tablespoon tomato paste, for color (optional)

Freshly ground black pepper to taste

¹/₄ cup chopped fresh parsley

¹/₄ cup chopped fresh basil or 1 teaspoon dried

1. In large, nonreactive pan, combine all ingredients except tomato paste, pepper, parsley, and fresh basil. If using dried basil, add now. Cook, uncovered, over medium heat for 20 to 25 minutes, or until tomatoes are soft and mixture is thick.

2. Remove bay leaf. Stir in tomato paste if desired. Season with pepper. Stir in fresh parsley and basil.

Makes 3 cups

Soups for All Seasons

At lunchtime, spas serve soups that are rich with beans, brimming with vegetables and flavored with herbs, spices and chilies. Some spa soups are simple and light; others are complex stews. Hot soups warm guests on chilly days, while cold soups refresh them when the temperatures climb.

There are many benefits to including soup in your diet year-round. First of all, it's easy to fix. You can make almost any kind in advance and keep it in your refrigerator, heating only the portion you want for each meal. If you have some extra time, you can make a low-fat soup stock and freeze it, using it as a base for freshly made soups or other dishes. Otherwise, low-fat, low-sodium broths are readily available in grocery stores.

Soup is also an excellent option for those who prefer meatless meals, and it makes a great melting pot for leftovers from a party or holiday feast. The remains of a Thanksgiving or Christmas turkey can easily be turned into a week of lunches simply by adding water, an array of vegetables like carrots, onion and celery, and your favorite spices.

To all these good reasons for including soup on your menu, spas add one more. They often use soup as a low-fat, flavorful sauce to liven up chicken, fish and rice dishes and as a simple casserole filler. At home, find your own inventive ways to expand your use of soup. Tomato-based varieties are best mixed with pasta or spooned on top of potatoes. Add beans, fish, spices and vegetables, and soup becomes a chili or a cioppino. Basic vegetable or chicken stock can be used instead of oil to make a pasta primavera or an oil-free stir-fry. Use soup regularly, and you'll soon find it's not only a delicious meal in its own right but at the core of a creative approach to more healthful cooking. Here are some recipes to get you started.

VEGETABLE BROTH
from the Golden Door

12 cups water

2 celery stalks

1 carrot

1 small leek with top

1 small onion, dotted with 4 to 5 whole cloves

1½ cups cabbage

1 cup parsley

½ cup fresh basil sprigs

1 sprig fresh thyme

1 bay leaf

2 teaspoons crushed black peppercorns

1 tablespoon coarse salt (optional)

1. Combine all ingredients in a large soup pot. Bring to a boil, reduce heat, and simmer for about 2 hours.
2. Strain.
Makes 8 to 9 cups
NOTE: Stock will keep for several days in the refrigerator or several weeks in the freezer.

CREAM OF MUSHROOM SOUP
from the Cooper Aerobics Center

1 tablespoon olive oil

1 medium onion, finely chopped

½ cup red wine

1 teaspoon dried basil, or more to taste

1 teaspoon dried thyme leaves, or more to taste

1 pound fresh button mushrooms, chopped

4 cups low-fat beef or chicken stock

2 tablespoons cornstarch mixed with ¼ cup cold water

1 package butter buds (dry, not reconstituted)

1½ cups evaporated skim milk

Pinch of white pepper

Pinch of nutmeg

1. Heat olive oil in a large saucepan that has been sprayed with nonstick cooking spray. Add onion and stir over moderate heat until onion begins to turn clear.

2. Add wine and simmer until onion is soft.

3. Add basil and thyme. Stir. Add mushrooms and cook for 5 minutes, stirring occasionally.

4. Add stock. Bring mixture to a boil. Add cornstarch mixture and butter buds. Return mixture to a boil. Reduce heat and simmer for 3 to 5 minutes.

5. Add evaporated milk, white pepper, and nutmeg. Adjust seasonings and thicken with more cornstarch until soup reaches desired consistency.

Makes about 8 cups

AUTHORS' NOTE: This also makes a wonderful clear soup made without the evaporated milk.

CREAM OF FRESH CORN SOUP

from the Golden Door

1 teaspoon canola oil

1/2 medium onion, diced

1 small carrot, sliced

1 bay leaf

1 teaspoon dried basil

5 medium ears white sweet corn, shucked and kernels cut from cob

5 cups Vegetable Broth (*see page 64*) or water

1 teaspoon ground white pepper

1/2 teaspoon kosher salt, optional

2 tablespoons snipped fresh chives

1. In a soup pot, heat canola oil over medium heat.

2. Add onion, carrot, bay leaf, and basil and sauté until onion is translucent. Stir in the corn and sauté for another 3 to 4 minutes. Add vegetable broth or water.

3. Reduce heat and simmer, uncovered, for 35

to 40 minutes. Remove from heat, discard bay leaf, and let cool.

4. Transfer soup to blender and blend until creamy. Strain through fine sieve, adding more broth if desired. Taste for seasoning and add salt if desired. Return to soup pot and heat through before serving. Garnish with chives.

Makes about 6 cups

AUTHORS' NOTE: This soup has a rich, golden color as well as a wonderful flavor.

CHILLED ASPARAGUS SOUP

from the ISPA Collaboration

1 tablespoon olive oil

1 pound asparagus, trimmed and broken into pieces

1/2 cup chopped onion

3 cups water or vegetable stock

1/2 cup skim milk

1/4 cup long-grain rice

Salt and ground black pepper to taste

4 teaspoons nonfat sour cream

1. In a large saucepan or soup pot, heat oil over low heat.

2. Add asparagus and onion. Cook until asparagus is tender, about 10 minutes. Do not allow to brown.

3. Add water or stock, milk, and rice. Cook for 45 minutes. Cool slightly.

4. In a food processor or blender, process mixture until smooth. Strain into bowl or container. Season with salt and pepper. Refrigerate. To serve, top each serving with 1/2 teaspoon sour cream.

Makes 3 cups

AUTHORS' NOTE: This soup is also very good hot. Strain, season, top with low-fat sour cream if desired, and serve.

CUISINE NATURELLE RED LENTIL CHILI

from Anara Spa at the Hyatt Regency Kauai

1 cup sliced carrots

¾ cup sliced zucchini

¾ cup sliced yellow squash

¾ cup diced eggplant

½ cup chopped onions

1 teaspoon olive oil

1½ cups red lentils

2 cups low-fat chicken stock or vegetable stock

1 bay leaf

1 teaspoon Mrs. Dash vegetable seasoning

2 teaspoons oregano

½ teaspoon cumin

½ teaspoon chili powder

¾ teaspoon cayenne pepper

¾ teaspoon ground nutmeg

¾ teaspoon finely chopped garlic

1 jalapeño, seeded and halved

3 pounds plum tomatoes, chopped

Blue corn tortillas to garnish

2 tablespoons plain nonfat yogurt

6 cilantro sprigs

1. In a food processor, chop carrots, zucchini, squash, eggplant, onion, and jalapeño halves until finely ground. In a deep sauté pan or stock pot, gently cook vegetable mixture in olive oil over medium heat for 5 minutes.
2. Add lentils, stock, dry seasonings, garlic, jalapeño and tomatoes. Simmer for 45 minutes.
3. Spray tortillas with nonstick cooking spray. In a skillet over medium heat, cook tortillas one at a time until crispy. Break into quarters.
4. Ladle chili into bowls. Garnish with tortilla chips and top with yogurt and cilantro sprigs.
Makes about 6 cups

ROASTED GREEN CHILE AND CHICKEN SOUP

from Lake Austin Spa Resort

6 cups low-fat chicken stock

2 cups tomatillos

1 bunch green onions, trimmed and cut into ½-inch lengths

1 small onion, coarsely chopped

3 cloves garlic, minced

1 tablespoon cumin

1 teaspoon sugar

⅓ cup cilantro, chopped, plus additional for garnish, if desired

4 New Mexican green chilies, roasted, peeled, seeded, and diced

A 4-ounce boneless, skinless chicken breast

2 red new potatoes, diced

1 cup diced tomato

1 zucchini, diced

2 tablespoons masa harina, dissolved in enough additional chicken stock to make a pourable paste

2 limes, cut into 6 wedges

1. Simmer the tomatillos, green onions, and onion in 2 cups of chicken stock for 5 minutes.
2. In a blender or food processor, puree tomatillo mixture, garlic, cumin, sugar, cilantro, and half of the diced chilies. Set aside.
3. Simmer the chicken breast in 4 cups of stock for 15 minutes. Remove the meat, reserving the stock. Let the meat cool, then shred.
4. Add the potatoes and tomato to the stock and simmer for 5 minutes. Add zucchini and cook for 1 minute.
5. Whisk in masa paste, cook for a couple of minutes, then add tomatillo mixture, reserved chicken, and remaining chilies.
6. Heat through. Serve with lime wedges and additional chopped cilantro.
Makes about 8 cups

GAZPACHO

from the ISPA Collaboration

1 bunch cilantro

1 red pepper, coarsely chopped

1 green pepper, coarsely chopped

1 cucumber, seeded and coarsely chopped

2 cups tomato juice

3 tomatoes, seeded and coarsely chopped

Juice of 1 lemon

Juice of 1 lime

1 tablespoon Tabasco sauce

Salt and ground black pepper to taste

1. Measure ¼ of the cilantro and finely chop.
2. In a small bowl, place chopped cilantro and ¼ each of red pepper, green pepper, and cucumber. Cover and refrigerate.
3. In a food processor or blender, process remaining cilantro, peppers, cucumber, tomato juice, and other ingredients until smooth. Strain into a large container or bowl. Cover and refrigerate for several hours or overnight.
4. Serve topped with chopped vegetable mixture.
Makes about 3 cups

▌ Satisfying Salads

Like soups, salads are a satisfying way to add vegetables to your diet. Spas serve some kind of salad at lunch daily, prepared with fresh greens and vegetables, often just picked from their own organic gardens. A small amount of cheese may be added for flavor. Chicken, fish or turkey is an accompaniment, not the centerpiece. You may find a low-fat slaw beside a burger or a slice of pizza, or sample a salad made with fruits such as apples, mangoes, papayas or grapes. Dressings are always homemade, often with fresh herbs, and are so inventive you'd never know they are missing the oil and fat of traditional dressings.

Many spas offer lunchtime salad bars filled with vegetables, beans and low-fat dressings. At a restaurant, on the other hand, the selections can be deceivingly high in fat. When faced with such an array, pile on the broccoli, cucumber and peppers, add some garbanzo beans or fruit, but be sparse with cheese, avocado and nuts, and avoid side dishes like potato salad and oil-marinated mushrooms. Go light on the dressings or pick low-fat varieties.

At home, it can be fun to create your own salads. Pile on your favorite greens, such as romaine, radicchio, arugula and spinach. These are so low in calories that some spa nutritionists don't even count them in guests' daily totals. Then add the vegetables you love best, whenever possible using those that are in season. Each week try adding a vegetable you've never eaten before—perhaps watercress, bean sprouts, purple peppers or yellow tomatoes.

With so many farmers markets and fresh produce stores to choose from today, it's not hard to make delicious, beautiful salads. For ways to make your lunch salads more creative, start with some of these spa specialties.

CHICKEN GRAPE SALAD

from the Cooper Aerobics Center

4 4-ounce boneless, skinless chicken breasts

1½ cups water

1 low-sodium bouillon cube

1½ cups seedless green grapes

¼ cup pecan halves

⅓ cup diced celery

⅓ cup chopped fresh dill

¼ cup low-fat sour cream

¼ cup low-fat mayonnaise

¼ teaspoon salt

¼ teaspoon ground black pepper

2 bunches watercress (optional)

Dill sprigs for garnish (optional)

1. Preheat over to 350°F.

2. Arrange the chicken breasts in a single layer in a shallow baking pan.

3. In a small saucepan, bring water to a boil and add the bouillon cube. Stir to dissolve. Pour enough bouillon in the baking pan to just cover the chicken breasts. Cover chicken with aluminum foil and bake until cooked through, about 20 minutes. Allow the chicken to cool in the liquid. Discard liquid after cooling.

4. Shred the chicken into bite-sized pieces and place in a large bowl. Add the grapes, pecans, celery, and chopped dill. Toss well.

5. In a separate bowl, mix the sour cream and mayonnaise. Toss into the chicken salad. Season with salt and pepper. Cover and refrigerate for 2 hours.

6. Serve on a bed of watercress or other salad greens, garnished with dill sprigs.

Makes 5 servings

FRESH ISLAND MANGO, ROASTED RED PEPPER, AND MAUI ONION SALAD

from Spa Grande at Grand Wailea Resort

2 Maui onions, or any sweet onions, sliced into ¼-inch-thick slices (leave skin on)

2 ripe mangoes or papayas, peeled and cut into large pieces

2 roasted red peppers, halved

1 cup basil (opal or green recommended), cut into strips

¼ cup balsamic vinegar

¼ cup extra-virgin olive oil

Freshly ground black pepper

1. Preheat oven to 350°F.

2. Caramelize the onions: Place them on a lightly oiled cookie sheet and bake for approximately 25 minutes, turning them once, or until they look "caramelly."

3. Arrange mangoes, peppers, and onions on four plates. Sprinkle with basil and drizzle with vinegar and oil. Sprinkle with black pepper.

Makes 4 servings

Inspired Low-Fat Dressings

Salad dressings are frequently the high-fat downfall of otherwise health-conscious eaters. Yet nothing could be simpler than to make low-fat dressings that are flavorful at the same time. Spa chefs use fruit and fruit juice to sweeten dressings and substitute balsamic vinegar or yogurt for oil. A wide array of herbs blend to give the dressings rich, varied tastes. You can experiment, as spa chefs do, and invent your own dressings, or try some of these spa favorites.

BALSAMIC VINAIGRETTE

from the Golden Door

$1/4$ **cup balsamic vinegar**

3 tablespoons spring water

2 tablespoons Dijon mustard

$1/2$ **teaspoon freshly ground black pepper**

2 tablespoons minced parsley

2 tablespoons olive oil

Whisk all ingredients until well blended.

Makes $1/2$ cup

RASPBERRY VINAIGRETTE

from the Golden Door

$2/3$ **cup fresh or frozen unsweetened raspberries**

1 tablespoon unsweetened apple juice or water

$1/4$ **cup raspberry vinegar**

3 tablespoons water

2 teaspoons fructose

2 teaspoons canola oil

$1/4$ **teaspoon freshly ground black pepper**

1. In a blender, briefly blend raspberries and apple juice. Strain through a fine sieve. (This should yield about $1/2$ cup raspberry puree.)

2. Add remaining ingredients to raspberry puree and whisk together.

Makes 1 cup

RUSSIAN POPPYSEED DRESSING

from the Doral Golf Resort and Spa

1 cup low-fat cottage cheese

$1/3$ **cup plain nonfat yogurt**

1 teaspoon Dijon mustard

2 teaspoons apple cider vinegar

1 $1/2$ tablespoons ketchup

2 tablespoons grated onion

Juice of $1/2$ lemon

1 teaspoon poppyseeds

1. In a blender, blend all ingredients until smooth.

2. Refrigerate for 2 hours to allow flavors to mingle.

Makes 1 $1/2$ cups

BUTTERMILK RANCH DRESSING

from the PGA National Resort and Spa

$1/2$ **cup low-fat cottage cheese**

$1/4$ **cup low-fat buttermilk**

2 tablespoons low-fat mayonnaise

2 tablespoons grated Parmesan cheese

1 tablespoon lemon juice

1 clove garlic, cut in pieces

1 shallot, chopped

1 teaspoon dried oregano

$1/2$ **teaspoon dried thyme**

$1/2$ **teaspoon freshly ground black pepper**

1. In a food processor or blender, puree all ingredients until smooth.

2. Refrigerate for at least 1 hour to allow flavors to mingle.

Makes 1 $1/4$ cups

(continued on page 70)

(continued from page 69)

DIJON MUSTARD DRESSING

from the ISPA Collaboration

1 cup low-fat cottage cheese

$1/3$ cup plain nonfat yogurt

1 teaspoon Dijon mustard

1 teaspoon dry mustard

1 teaspoon Worcestershire sauce

1 teaspoon A-1 steak sauce

2 teaspoons evaporated skim milk

1. Place all ingredients in a blender and blend until smooth.

2. Refrigerate for 2 hours to allow flavors to mingle.

Makes 2$1/4$ cups

LEMON LAVENDER DRESSING

from the ISPA Collaboration

$1/4$ cup lemon juice

$1/4$ cup orange juice

$1/4$ cup raspberry vinegar

1 tablespoon olive oil

2 teaspoons fresh lavender

Salt and ground black pepper to taste

In a food processor or blender, puree all ingredients until well combined.

Makes about 1 cup

APPLE CABBAGE SLAW VERONICA

from the ISPA Collaboration

$1 1/2$ cups finely shredded cabbage

$1/2$ cup chopped orange segments

$1/2$ cup halved seedless grapes

$1/2$ cup diced red apple

$1/4$ cup thinly sliced celery

$1/2$ cup plain nonfat yogurt

$1/2$ teaspoon grated lemon peel

$1/2$ teaspoon lemon juice

$1/2$ teaspoon honey

6 lettuce leaves for garnish

1. In a large bowl, mix cabbage, orange, grapes, apple, and celery.

2. In a small bowl, stir together yogurt, lemon peel, lemon juice, and honey.

3. Pour yogurt mixture over cabbage mixture. Toss gently to coat evenly.

4. Serve immediately, on lettuce leaves if desired.

Makes 6 servings

HOT SPINACH SALAD

from the ISPA Collaboration

$1/4$ cup thinly sliced red onion

1 tablespoon chopped garlic

1 tablespoon olive oil

$3/4$ cup sliced mushrooms

$1/3$ cup balsamic vinegar

1 roasted red pepper, cut into strips

$1/2$ cup snow peas, sliced crosswise in thirds

1 pound fresh spinach, trimmed, washed, and dried

1. In a medium skillet over high heat, sauté onion and garlic in oil for 2 minutes.

2. Add mushrooms and vinegar. Reduce heat to low. Simmer until mushrooms and onions are tender.

3. Add roasted pepper and snow peas. Cook over high heat for 1 minute.

4. Remove from heat and toss with spinach in a large bowl until spinach is well coated.

5. Serve immediately on warm plates.

Makes 2 servings

INSALATA TRICOLORE ZENZERO
from the ISPA Collaboration

Juice from 5 oranges (about 1 1/3 cups)

1 tablespoon grated fresh ginger

1/4 cup Champagne vinegar

2 tablespoons minced shallots

2 tablespoons peanut oil

Salt to taste

White pepper to taste

2 fennel bulbs, cut into julienne strips

3 heads radicchio, torn into small pieces

3 oranges, peeled and sectioned

1. Place orange juice and ginger in a small saucepan over low heat. Cook until mixture has a syrupy consistency. Stir in vinegar and shallots.

2. Whisk in oil, salt, and pepper until well blended.

3. Place fennel and radicchio in a large bowl. Add half of the dressing and the orange sections. Toss until well coated. Serve immediately, with remaining dressing on the side.

Makes 6 servings

Nutritious Salad Greens

Whenever you are making salads at home, make the most of your greens. Remember that the freshest will always be the most nutritious. If you buy lettuce or greens sealed in a bag, it is best to use them within four or five days. Baby greens are generally easier to digest. Bitter greens carry the most nutrients. Iceberg, romaine and butter lettuce are mostly water but still provide important fiber.

With so many selections available at produce markets, it should be easy to find greens you like. Here are some suggestions for nutritious, tasty greens offered by Spa Grande at the Grand Hyatt Wailea Resort in Maui, Hawaii:

ARUGULA — A spicy, slightly peppery salad green that first grew wild throughout the Mediterranean.

AMARANTH — Also called Chinese spinach, amaranth is prized for its high protein content, delicious spinach-like flavor and delicate, fern-like foliage. It was traditionally believed to have rejuvenating qualities.

CRESS — Garden, golden and common cress have fine, textured leaves and a peppery flavor.

DANDELION — Rich in vitamins and minerals, this pungent green is best eaten young, before the plant flowers.

FRISÉE — A kind of chicory, frisée has a slightly bitter taste that offsets the sweetness of mild lettuces and is complemented by fruity vinegars.

RADICCHIO — Another form of chicory, this red and white Italian lettuce is tangy and slightly bitter and has become very popular in America in recent years.

BELGIAN ENDIVE — This delicate and slightly bitter green grows as the root of the Whitloof chicory. It comes in heads of crisp, pale, tightly furled leaves.

▌Eating Out: Cuisines of the World

While some ethnic cuisines have come under fire for their megadoses of fat and calories, you just need to know what to order to have a perfectly acceptable lunch from any cuisine in the world. In fact, ethnic cuisines such as Japanese, Indian and Thai are often filled with the vegetables, lean meat, poultry and fish recommended for a healthful lunch. If you choose wisely, herbs and spices in place of salt and fat, can add tremendous flavor and make meals exotic as well as nutritious. Here arc some suggestions from the Doral Golf Resort and Spa, Canyon Ranch and PGA for common ethnic entrées to order and avoid.

Chinese Cuisine

Order Chicken and rice soup, hot-and-sour soup, sizzling rice soup, wonton soup, stir-fried chicken, steamed Peking rolls, steamed vegetables, vegetable chop suey, Hunan spicy chicken, mu shu vegetables, moo goo gai pan, minced chicken or squab in lettuce leaves, teriyaki chicken or beef skewer, sizzling sliced chicken, tofu or bean curd, roasted or twice-cooked pork, chicken or vegetable lo mein, white rice, steamed dumplings or dim sum, soft noodles, fruit, fortune cookies.

Avoid Egg drop soup, fried rice, fried wontons, fried shrimp, egg foo young, chicken with cashews, kung pao chicken, egg and spring rolls, spareribs, sweet and sour duck, volcano shrimp, soy sauce.

Japanese Cuisine

Order Miso soup, suimono (clear broth), noodle soups, sunomono, tofu salad, boiled spinach, sushi or sashimi, California and other rolls, teriyaki, shabu-shabu (sliced beef with vegetables and noodles), sukiyaki chicken or beef, tataki (seared tuna), yakitori (grilled chicken), steamed brown or white rice, daikon (radish), ginger, yaki-soba (buckwheat noodles), fresh fruit.

Avoid Smoked eel, tempura, agemono (battered and fried items), fried bean curd, fried soft-shelled crab, unagi (broiled eel), katsu (deep-fried pork), fried ice cream, yo kan (sweet bean cake), sake.

Mexican Cuisine

Order Black bean soup, gazpacho, seviche (marinated seafood), chili con carne, mixed green or vegetable salad, corn tortillas, salsa, arroz con pollo (chicken with rice), chicken or shrimp fajitas, chicken or bean enchiladas (no cheese), soft chicken tacos, steamed tamales, grilled chicken salad, chicken or fish marinated in lime, Mexican rice, black or red beans, refried beans (no lard), fruit.

Avoid Nachos, guacamole and chips, refried beans (with lard), fried chimichangas, chili con queso, sour cream enchiladas, tostadas, chili rellenos, fried burritos, mole sauce, carnitas, chorizo, flan.

Italian Cuisine

Order Minestrone soup, zuppa de pesce (fish soup), pasta e fagioli (pasta and bean soup), mixed green salad, marinated calamari or mushrooms, tomato and onion salad, roasted pepper salad, tuna and bean salad, steamed clams, grilled or broiled seafood, chicken marsala, fruitti di mare, pasta with marinara sauce, seafood or chicken primavera, cioppino, linguini with red or white clam sauce, chicken cacciatore, pizza with vegetable toppings, Italian ice, fruit, anise cookies, biscotti.

Avoid Garlic bread, fonduta, prosciutto, Caesar salad, bruschetta (garlic bread with olive oil), pasta with cream sauces such as Alfredo, stuffed cheese pasta, fried zucchini and calamari, cannelloni, pesto sauce, marsala sauce, veal Parmigiana, tiramisu, zabaglione.

Indian Cuisine

Order Mulligatawny (tomato-based lentil soup), dahl rasam (pepper soup with lentils), raita (cucumber and yogurt), dahl (lentils), tamata salat (diced tomatoes and onions), aloo chole (garbanzo beans with tomato and potato), basmati rice, tandoori chicken or fish, chicken vindaloo (hot spices), yogurt-based curry dishes, shrimp bhuna (cooked with vegetables), naan (baked bread), mango or mint chutney, fruit.

Avoid Gulabjamuns (fried milk balls), ghee (clarified butter), samosa (fried vegetable turnover), shrimp malai, beef or lamb dishes, vegetable korma (cooked with cream and nuts), poori and paratha (fried breads), koulfi (ice cream with nuts).

Thai Cuisine

Order Steamed white rice, seafood, yum nuan salad (mixed vegetables), any clear soup, hot-and-spicy soup, lemon grass soup, ginger-steamed fish, spicy ground chicken breast, chicken in roasted curry sauce, garlic pepper chicken, hang mung poo (spicy steamed mussels), seafood with chili tomato sauce, chicken in red curry paste, chicken saté, ramutan (fruit), lychee nuts.

Avoid Fried rice, anything made with coconut milk, peanut sauces, anything deep fried, crispy noodles, pork dishes, squid, coconut ice cream or pudding, Thai custard.

French Cuisine

Order Consommé, French onion soup (without cheese), pistou (vegetable soup), bouillabaisse, steamed mussels, mixed green salad, salad Niçoise, artichokes, hearts of palm and white asparagus, poached chicken, coq au vin (chicken in wine sauce), pot-au-feu (chicken in broth), roasted chicken, broiled sole, fish en papillote, quenelles, stewed rabbit, ratatouille, French bread (no butter), grilled vegetables, fruit, sorbets, meringue shells with fruit.

Avoid Cream soups or bisques, creamy cheeses, saucissons (sausage), anything en croute, brioche or croissants, veal française, duck, organ meats, rack of lamb, escargot, Napoleons, crème brûlée, souffles.

Greek and Middle Eastern Cuisine

Order Lentil soup, pita bread, tomato and cucumber salad, fattoush (salad of bread, cucumbers, tomatoes, green peppers), Greek salad, tabbouleh salad, beef, chicken or vegetable shish kebab, lemon chicken, dolma (grape leaves stuffed with rice and vegetables), baked eggplant, couscous, plaki (fish with vegetables), baba ghanoush (pureed eggplant), hummus (pureed chickpeas), fruit, rice pudding.

Avoid Fried cheese, gyro or souvlaki, moussaka (eggplant, cheese, ground meat, béchamel sauce), kibbeh (lamb and butter), spanokopita (spinach pie), fried falafel, fried pastries.

▮ Cooking at Home, Ethnic-Style

When you cook ethnic-style at home, it's even easier to cut fat and calories because you have complete control of the ingredients. Spa chefs love to cook ethnic-style food and invent many exotic-sounding recipes that aren't difficult to make. Here are some favorite spa recipes you may want to try the next time you're in the mood for an exotic lunch.

EGGPLANT ENCHILADAS

from Lake Austin Spa Resort

1 cup chopped onion

2 cloves garlic, minced

$1/2$ cup low-fat chicken broth

6 cups (about 2 small) peeled, cubed eggplant

1 cup chopped green pepper

1 cup sliced fresh mushrooms

1 teaspoon Worcestershire sauce

2 tablespoons chopped toasted almonds

1 tablespoon minced fresh parsley

1 teaspoon freshly ground black pepper

1 cup grated low-fat Monterey Jack cheese

12 whole-wheat flour tortillas

1. Preheat oven to 350°F. Spray a glass baking dish with nonstick cooking spray.

2. In a large skillet over medium heat, cook onion and garlic in $1/4$ cup stock over medium heat for 5 minutes. Stir in eggplant, green pepper, mushrooms, and Worcestershire sauce.

3. Cook for 10 to 12 minutes, or until eggplant is soft. Remove from heat. Add almonds, parsley, black pepper, and $3/4$ cup of the cheese.

4. Simmer $1/4$ cup of stock in a small frying pan. One by one, dip tortillas in pan, turning once, to soften. Place a portion of the eggplant mixture in each tortilla and roll tightly. Place seam side down in baking dish. Top with remaining cheese and bake for 20 minutes.

Makes 12 servings

AUTHORS' NOTE: If you like creamier enchiladas, add more liquid or extra cheese.

SESAME TOFU STIR-FRY

from the ISPA Collaboration

$1/4$ cup lite soy sauce

2 tablespoons dry sherry

$1 1/2$ tablespoons minced ginger

$1 1/2$ tablespoons minced garlic

2 pounds firm tofu, well drained and cut into 1-inch cubes

1 teaspoon peanut oil

2 large onions, sliced

3 cups diagonally sliced celery

3 cups diagonally sliced broccoli

3 cups mung bean sprouts, rinsed and well drained

3 cups sliced mushrooms

$1/2$ tablespoon arrowroot

4 cups cooked brown rice

2 tablespoons sesame seeds, toasted

1. In a shallow casserole or bowl, mix soy sauce, sherry, and $1/2$ tablespoon each of ginger and garlic. Add tofu and marinate.

2. In a large skillet or wok, heat peanut oil over high heat. Add remaining ginger and garlic. Add onions, celery, broccoli, bean sprouts, and mushrooms. Cook, stirring constantly, until vegetables are crisp-tender. If mixture begins to stick, add a splash of sherry.

3. Remove tofu from marinade. Put marinade in a small bowl. Stir in arrowroot until well combined. Add to skillet.

4. Reduce heat to medium. Cook, stirring constantly, until mixture is thickened.

5. Reduce heat to low. Add tofu. Cover and simmer for 2 to 3 minutes.

6. To serve, divide rice among plates. Top with tofu-vegetable mixture and a sprinkle of sesame seeds.

Makes 8 servings

WILD RICE STIR-FRY
from the ISPA Collaboration

1 tablespoon peanut oil

1 pound pork tenderloin, cut in 16 strips

1 cup diagonally sliced celery

1 cup diagonally sliced green onion

1 cup sliced mushrooms

An 8-ounce can sliced water chestnuts, drained

1 cup fresh or frozen snow peas

1 teaspoon grated fresh ginger

2 cups cooked wild rice

3 tablespoons lite soy sauce

1 tablespoon cornstarch

1 tablespoon dry sherry

$^1/_2$ teaspoon salt (optional)

1. In a large skillet or wok, heat peanut oil over high heat. Add pork strips. Cook, stirring constantly, for 2 minutes.

2. Add celery, green onion, mushrooms, water chestnuts, snow peas, and ginger. Cook, stirring constantly, for about 5 minutes, until vegetables are crisp-tender.

3. Add wild rice. Toss until well combined.

4. In a small bowl, stir soy sauce, cornstarch, sherry, and salt until blended. Add to vegetable-rice mixture. Cook, stirring, until thickened.

Makes 6 servings

CHICKEN SATÉ WITH SPA PEANUT SAUCE
from the PGA National Resort and Spa

2 pounds boneless, skinless chicken breast, cut into 32 thin strips

2 tablespoons lime juice

2 teaspoons honey

2 teaspoons ground coriander

Spa Peanut Sauce (*see below*)

1. Soak bamboo skewers in water for 2 hours.

2. In a medium bowl, toss chicken strips with lime juice, honey, and coriander. Marinate in refrigerator for at least 30 minutes or overnight.

3. Preheat grill or broiler.

4. Thread each piece of chicken on a bamboo skewer. Grill or broil until cooked through, turning once.

5. Serve with warm Spa Peanut Sauce.

Makes 8 servings

SPA PEANUT SAUCE

$^1/_2$ cup peanut butter

1 tablespoon lime juice

2 tablespoons low-fat chicken broth or stock

1 tablespoon honey

1 teaspoon vegetable oil

$^1/_4$ teaspoon minced fresh ginger

1. Bring all ingredients to a boil over medium heat, stirring constantly.

2. Cool slightly. Serve warm.

Makes 1 cup

INDIAN SWEET AND SOUR BEAN CASSEROLE

from the ISPA Collaboration

1 teaspoon extra-virgin olive oil

1/2 pound cabbage, sliced

1 medium carrot, peeled and sliced

1 small leek, cleaned and sliced

1 medium red pepper, seeded and sliced

1 1/2 cups hot vegetable broth

2 cups cooked chickpeas

1 medium apple, cored and coarsely chopped

1 medium banana, cut into small pieces

1 to 2 cloves garlic, minced

1/2 teaspoon ground ginger

1/2 teaspoon ground coriander

1 teaspoon apple cider vinegar

1 teaspoon lite soy sauce

Salt to taste

1 teaspoon chopped almonds

1. Place oil, cabbage, and carrots in a large saucepan or soup pot and cook for 5 minutes over medium heat.

2. Add leek and pepper. Cook for 2 minutes.

3. Add broth, chickpeas, apple, banana, garlic, ginger, and coriander. Cook for 10 minutes. Stir and cook for 10 minutes more.

4. Mix in vinegar, soy sauce, and salt. Remove from heat.

5. Serve topped with almonds. If desired, serve over rice or potatoes, with sliced bananas, chutney, and raisins on the side.

Makes 4 servings

Reality Check

Build on Your Own Foundation

When making changes to your diet, it's not necessary to throw out everything you normally eat and start all over again. Instead, use your current diet as a foundation and build on it with nutritious foods you like. Instead of just thinking about what you *shouldn't* eat, think of all the foods you can add to make your meals more healthful and more interesting. There is no perfect way to eat, only ways of eating better.

COMING TO YOUR SENSES

Lunch is over, it's early in the afternoon and the highlight of your day is just ahead. You've challenged your body with exercise and replenished it with healthful food. Now it's time to put yourself in someone else's hands. After changing into a robe and slippers, you are led to a wonderfully scented, warm waiting room where soft music plays in the background. Soon a therapist comes to lead you to a private room for your first treatment of the day. Perhaps you've chosen a skin-cleansing salt glow and mineral bath, an aromatherapy massage or an herbal wrap. Whatever it is, you're leaving the world behind and entering an environment in which everything has been designed to please your senses. Lie back, relax and let someone else take care of you. This time is your reward for all your hard work, and you're going to love it.

Beauty and body treatments may be the most loved and least understood aspect of a spa visit, enjoyed for their sensuousness and, at the same time, dismissed as frivolous and self-indulgent. At spas, however, these methods of taking care of your body are considered just as important for your overall well-being as anything else in your day. Massages, scrubs, baths, wraps and facials are all time-honored techniques for stimulating your body's natural processes of self-renewal. They are also beneficial for easing the effects of stress on your body and mind. On top of everything, they make you feel beautiful.

There is something magical about the transformation brought about in spa treatment rooms, probably because you are affected on so many levels by so many elements all at one time. Taking time out to recline in a warm place with pleasing scents and lulling sounds is an invitation to relax. The attention to your body and senses by another person is very nurturing, and caring hands satisfy a natural "skin hunger," or desire to be touched. Even the belief that you are doing something to make yourself beautiful can help your inner beauty emerge. All these elements, along with cleansing of skin, relaxation of musles, and stimulation of circulation, powerfully combine to release tension and help you look and feel better.

At spas, where ultra-relaxing treatments are given daily, you may experience an incredible transformation in only a few days. You blossom quickly under such nurturing, becoming more in tune with your senses and more at ease in your own skin. At home, you may be someone who constantly gives all your attention to others, leaving no one, including yourself, to take care of you. That needs to change. By setting aside as little as one day each month or one hour each week as "me" time and using it to develop a renewing ritual that makes you feel good, you can make great strides on your own. Just by doing this much for yourself—and it's amazing how many people don't—you can shed some of the effects of stressful living and rediscover a more relaxed and positive outlook on life.

It's true that spas have the advantage of having trained therapists and specialized equipment. And there's no question that having someone else take care of you is an important part of the experience, especially if you aren't in the habit of caring for yourself. It will help if you can treat yourself to an occasional morning or afternoon at a resort, hotel or day spa in your area. Here, you can get ideas for ways to simulate the spa environment at home.

Even more important, trying the full experience first can help you discover the state of deep relaxation you want to achieve when you do treatments on your own and help you understand what the effects of treatments should be. Spas such as Hotel Crescent Court and the Four Seasons Resort and Club, both in Dallas, the Spa at the Houstonian in Houston, the Claremont Resort and Spa in Berkeley, California, and the Peninsula Hotel and Spa in New York City, all have a full array of treatments and top therapists, are open to the public and make wonderful day, afternoon or even lunch-hour retreats.

Even without access to a day spa, there are many ways to design self-renewal rituals at home. It isn't difficult to learn a few basic techniques for cleansing and relaxing, and it's easy to find products and other resources that can help. With a little imagination and a willingness to spend the time, you can develop the rituals that best suit your tastes.

One of the best and easiest ways is to expand on a typical bath or shower. Water has always been at the heart of the spa experience. European spas were developed around mineral springs where people came to soak away ailments and to relax and socialize. Even though springs are not an essential component of contemporary American spas, baths and other water treatments still abound. There are amazingly inventive ways of tapping into the capacity of water to cleanse, warm, cool, support and naturally massage your body.

At the Broadmoor in Colorado Springs, for example, European-style hydrotherapy includes multiple-head Swiss showers that alternately spray hot and cold water, a Scotch hose for a fire-hose-style spray massage and a Vichy shower that sprays softly while you are lying on a bench. At Spa Grande at the Grand Wailea in Maui, Hawaii, every treatment from facials to massages begins with a circuit of mud, seaweed and aromatherapy baths, while at the PGA National Resort and Spa in Palm Beach Gardens, Florida, outdoor soaking pools are filled with mineral salts imported from such renowned therapeutic sites as the Dead Sea.

Other spas use baths as a way to give guests a flavor of the locale. Those located seaside, such as Ihilani Resort and Spa in Oahu, Hawaii, and Gurney's Inn in Montauk, New York, use seawater to create "thalassotherapy" baths. Both Ihilani and Anara Spa on Hawaii's island of Kauai offer baths with mud that comes from one sacred site in Hawaii. By adding minerals mined in the nearby desert, even landlocked spas, such as Green Valley Spa and Tennis Resort in St. George, Utah, are able to link the bathing experience to the natural environment.

No matter where you live, the most important ingredient in any hydrotherapy treatment is water. As long as you have a standard bathtub, you can create a spalike experience at home. Turn off the phone and shut out the world to give yourself time without interruptions. Make the atmosphere as relaxing as possible. Dim the lights, burn a scented candle, turn on some calming music and set out some fluffy towels and a robe. Then draw a warm bath and add some aromatic oils, herbal blends, soothing muds or muscle-relaxing salts, depending on the effect you want. Lie back, close your eyes and let the warmth and buoyancy of the water melt away stress. You can refresh yourself in as little as twenty minutes, and if you add some time to rest afterward, the effect will be even better.

Though it isn't absolutely necessary, using one of the enormous number of spa-type products on the market today will add to any home treatment. Sometimes just the scent or feel of a new product can transform your experience. All spas use wonderfully luxurious creams, exfoliants, cleansers, oils and salts in their treatments, and guests can purchase many of them right there.

Sometimes spas import products from regions around the world, such as fango mud from Italy and seaweed from France. Others prefer using indigenous ingredients. The Peaks at Telluride, Colorado, uses high-alpine wild strawberries in an exfoliant, while Green Valley makes lotions from desert plants. Even if you never leave home, you can find products that evoke everything from rain forests to English gardens.

Some spa treatments are easier to simulate than others, while some of the most complex are nearly impossible to duplicate at home. Massage, by far the most popular treatment at spas, may be the most difficult to add to your home ritual without professional help, but it's not impossible. A simple prop, such as a smooth stone, can be applied to key spots on arms, legs, hands or feet for an experience similar to the hot-stone massage given at Miraval

Life in Balance in Tucson. Even without props, you can massage parts of your body that are easy to reach. If you can find a willing partner, you'll only need to learn a few basic strokes before you can take turns giving massages to each other. A full-body massage is wonderful, but an easy head, foot or hand rub can be just as relaxing.

When nothing but a professional massage will do, it's easy to locate licensed massage therapists who work out of an office or will come to your home for a visit. Once you start getting regular massages, you may never stop. It is unbeatable for relieving the tightness in neck, shoulder and back muscles induced by stressful living or the aches brought on by vigorous exercise. Perhaps even more than other body treatments, massage is a way of giving yourself over to the care of someone else. That nurturing touch may be the best tonic of all for your spirit.

As you become more familiar with spa treatments and what they involve, you can begin to integrate these self-renewal rituals into your life on a regular basis. Besides setting aside a time every week or month, you may want to set up a special spa day to share with friends. Experiment with beauty recipes, new products, enticing scents, pleasing colors and relaxing sounds. Find out what makes you respond positively. Develop new beauty and body routines as you get more experienced. Above all, enjoy yourself. Discovering what makes you feel good about your body is important. Getting in touch with the sensuous side of your life provides a much-needed balance in stressful times and will give you renewed energy and enthusiasm for daily living.

> **"Take care of yourself. If you don't, who will?"**
> Kathy Driscoll, owner, the Spa at the Houstonian

How to Use a Day Spa

Spas are famous for treatments with descriptive titles, such as "Botanical Detoxification Therapy," "Crushed Pearl Body Rub" and "De-Stress Aromatherapy Massage." Whether or not you understand exactly what they mean, the names alone conjure images of elaborate pampering that will leave you rested and beautified for months to come.

During a multiday visit to a spa, staff members generally help you set your schedule and explain what the treatments are and how they work. If you have only an hour or an afternoon to visit a day, resort or hotel spa, knowing in advance what is included in some of these complicated-sounding treatments helps avoid confusion and, in some cases, duplication. For example, body polishes and baths often incorporate some kind of massage. If

that's the case, you may not need or want to sign up for a massage afterward. Carefully read the description of the spa's services and when in doubt, ask. A few basic decoding skills can also set you in the right direction.

No matter how exotic it sounds, every treatment is a way to enhance your body's natural cleansing and renewing processes, such as circulation and perspiration. Depending on precisely how it stimulates your body, the treatment can be categorized as a scrub, a wrap, hydrotherapy (water treatment) or massage. Salon services, such as facials, hair and scalp treatments and hand and foot treatments tend to fall into a separate category, but they really rely on the same methods as full-body treatments. All treatments may be administered singly or in various combinations. The following guide explains various treatments and will help you interpret the colorful descriptions and understand what results to expect.

Scrubs These are treatments in which a gritty substance such as salt or crushed pearls is applied to your body and then rubbed or scrubbed off, generally with a brush or loofah. Sometimes a dry brush is applied directly to the skin.

Scrubs exfoliate dead skin, speeding up your body's natural skin-shedding process, and enhance circulation to the skin's surface. They leave your skin smoother and softer.

How to recognize a scrub: Look for words such as *glow, brush, smoother* and *rub*. Scrubs may also be called: body scrub, salt glow, loofah scrub, dry brush, skin glow, pearl polish, body polish, exfoliation, dulse scrub, gommage, body rub.

Wraps Sometimes called body masks, these are treatments in which you lie still and rest while your body is covered, or cocooned, with warm linens or plastic and foil. Often your skin will first be coated with a mud poultice or a substance such as paraffin wax or seaweed paste that is thought to nourish the skin.

Since you are kept very warm during the process, wraps encourage perspiration and also promote deep relaxation.

How to recognize a wrap: Usually the word *wrap* is used along with a descriptive term such as *detoxification, botanical, herbal, honey, paraffin, ti leaf, seaweed, aloe, fango, mud* or *moor mud.* On occasion, the word *wrap* is replaced with *mask, masque* or *pack.*

Hydrotherapy Since *hydro* means "water," you may assume that hydrotherapy treatments involve water, usually in the form of a bath or special shower. These treatments may include whirlpool or soaking baths with added oils, mineral salts or mud or showers with multinozzled jet shower heads, waterfall-like fountains or high-pressure hoses. Often hydrotherapy treatments include both. The water temperature ranges from warm to cool, and many therapies include a combination of the two. When *thalasso* is in the name, seawater or seaweed is involved.

Water therapies powerfully stimulate body temperature and blood circulation. They are very good at helping to relax stiff, sore muscles and easing other aches and pains. Warm baths, with their buoyant qualities, are especially calming.

How to recognize hydrotherapy: *Hydro* is often used in the description, though these kinds of treatments may also be called balneotherapy or thalassotherapy. Other phrases: aromabath, mineral bath, Roman bath, Vichy shower, Scotch hose, Swiss shower.

Massage These treatments are hands-on manipulations of muscles, connective tissue and joints. In general, Western-style massage is a full-body rubdown that is oriented toward muscle relaxation and stress relief, while Eastern styles focus on pressure points that stimulate energy. Massage also enhances blood circulation.

Some styles of massage are vigorous, others use light touch and many mix a variety of techniques. There are also massages that focus on specific body parts such as hands, feet or head. Body work that relies on gentle touch and energy sensing is also grouped with massage at spas.

How to recognize a massage: Swedish massage, a muscle relaxation technique that is offered almost everywhere, is the classic Western-style massage. Sports and deep-tissue massages are more vigorous forms of Western-style massages. Shiatsu is the best-known of the Eastern-style pressure-point massages. Other specialized massage and body work you may find: aromatherapy (the use of essential oils to aid in relaxation), lymph drainage (stimulates lymph circulation), reflexology (works pressure points on the feet), lomi-lomi (a Hawaiian massage that combines muscle-relaxing and pressure-point techniques) and Polarity, Reiki and cranial-sacral (all forms of energy-enhancing body work).

Facials These treatments for the face, as well as those for the scalp and hair, hands and feet, usually include cleansing and exfoliating, steam or heat, a mask and light massage.

Facials leave the skin clean and supple. They also promote blood circulation and can be very relaxing. Though treatments for the face and extremities are usually considered beauty routines, they are also good ways to relax parts of the body in which stress is frequently carried.

How to recognize a facial: European facials are the most common kind. Otherwise, facials are named according to their purpose: deep cleansing, deep pore, collagen, rejuvenating, revitalizing, hydrating or aromatherapy. Scalp and hair treatments often combine hot oil and massage, while hand and foot treatments may be included with manicures and pedicures.

Maximizing Your Day Spa Time

A half day or more If you want to have more than one treatment in a day, there is a logical order to follow. Try to schedule a scrub first, followed by a wrap or bath, then a massage. This way, your skin is cleansed first, allowing it to be more receptive to oils or other moisturizing substances. A bath or wrap is warming and relaxing, making you more receptive to the touch of massage. If possible, leave the replenishing oils from the massage on your body for as long as possible. If you plan to have a facial as well, be sure to schedule it after all other treatments to avoid showering off creams and oils.

Often you'll find combinations of scrubs,

wraps or baths and massages rolled into one treatment. Look for names like "Total Body Rejuvenator," "The Complete Treatment" or "The Rebalancer." These combined versions are good ways to experience a little bit of everything.

Making the most of one treatment

With time or money for only one treatment, most people choose massage. However, baths and other water treatments have soothing and relaxing qualities that can be equally beneficial and often include massage from a hose or underwater jets. If you do decide on a massage, be sure to arrive early enough to shower and unwind in a steam or sauna room beforehand.

Quick de-stressers

If you're very short on time or want to try something different, go for a hand, foot or hair and scalp treatment. Often overlooked in favor of whole-body treatments, these destressers focus on specific areas and can be wonderfully relaxing and invigorating. Foot (reflexology) and hand, neck and shoulder massages are all good stress-relieving choices, as are manicures, pedicures and hot-oil hair treatments that incorporate massage. In short, they are fast, easy ways to make yourself feel great.

Creating a Renewing Ritual

Taking time for yourself is easy at a spa. There, you don't have kids, jobs, friends and community obligations all vying for your attention. Spas are cocoons of safety, places to go to avoid burnout, where you can focus all your energy on your own well-being without feeling guilty or conflicted. A spa is a unique environment, where you feel as if you've stepped out of time and left the world behind. You know you'll be well taken care of. When you leave, you carry home a new outlook on life. You feel special again and refreshed for weeks afterward.

One way to recreate that feeling at home is by developing rituals in which you take care of yourself and your body. By taking time and learning how to create a space for yourself at home, you can turn the simplest body care into a ritual of self-renewal.

▮ **Take the time.** *Consider taking time a necessity, not a luxury. Time for yourself, even if it's only half an hour, can be restorative in itself. There may be a time in your day or week that already works well as a natural "down time"; if not, schedule it just as you would any other important obligation.*

▮ **Find a retreat.** *Once you've carved out the time, close the door on the world and escape to a quiet place where you can be alone. If you have a bath or a facial in mind, the bathroom makes sense. You can also cordon off a section of your bedroom with a pretty screen or find a corner where you can rest undisturbed. Let your family know that during this time you are "off limits."*

▮ **Add elements that make you happy.** *Everything you see, touch, smell and hear will have an effect on your experience and may help or hinder your level of relaxation. In the treatment areas of spas, the light is soft, the music lulling and the scent aromatic. You can easily duplicate this ambience at home by dimming the lights or*

reverie. Thoughts and images may seem to flow randomly. Let it happen. This state of mind is not only very restful but one in which creative ideas incubate. At the end of your time-out you'll feel mentally and physically refreshed.

■ **Come back slowly.** *Allow plenty of time to make the transition from your ritual to normal life. Be sure you've had time to cool off after a hot bath or steam and have taken time to rest. At spas, resting rooms occasionally contain poetry or inspirational writings to read during moments when your mind is receptive and relaxed. Allow yourself the same opportunity before you leave your retreat. Arrange your schedule so that you don't have to go into full speed immediately. By taking time to savor the way you feel, you give yourself a chance to complete the renewal process.*

■ Care and Feeding of Your Skin

Great skin always has a healthy-looking glow that reflects the time and effort you devote to it. It's not surprising, therefore, that many spa treatments are aimed at showing guests the best ways to take care of their skin. Beautiful skin is clean, moist and supple. To give it those qualities, spas use scrubs, wraps and facials. Some of these treatments are better left to trained therapists, while many are easy to duplicate at home. Everyone who wants to maintain a healthy-looking glow to their skin can benefit from adopting spalike treatments to supplement a regular skin-care regimen.

choosing a place with natural light, adding a scented candle or a vase of flowers and playing music conducive to your mood. You might even evoke a favorite place, like the mountains or the seashore, through colors, scents, natural objects and pictures that remind you of that environment. Make your retreat as inviting as you possibly can. As you begin to relax, your senses may become heightened—even more reason to surround yourself with things you find pleasurable. By creating a place of tranquility and beauty, your ritual will become more renewing than you ever thought possible.

■ **Let your mind go.** *As your body starts to relax during rest, bath or treatment, you may find yourself drifting into a half-awake/half-asleep*

Scrubs

Scrubs are cleansing whole-body treatments that are usually done prior to baths or wraps. They exfoliate—remove dead skin—to improve skin texture and stimulate circulation to leave you invigorated and refreshed. Scrubs are the easiest treatments to duplicate at home, since all you need is a loofah or even a washcloth and an exfoliant to spread on your body. Spa therapists may use ground salts, an aromatic body product unique to their spa, pumice or even something as exotic as crushed pearls. The exfoliant is spread all over your body and then rubbed off with a silk glove or a loofah. If you don't have an exfoliant product from a spa or beauty boutique at home, you can use a simple cornmeal and milk mixture or even a coarse salt softened with oil. Rub gently (rough rubbing can damage skin) in a circular motion, starting at your feet and moving upward along your body to your neck. Rinse thoroughly in a shower afterward. Bear in mind that a mild scrub once a week is preferable to an aggressive one less frequently.

The Dry Brush Alternative

An alternative to a scrub in the shower with loofahs and exfoliants is dry body brushing, which requires only a natural bristle brush. Body brushing is also a wonderful refresher, and you can do it even if you don't have time to shower or bathe. At Lake Austin Spa Resort in Austin, Texas, therapists teach guests this simple technique and even include a take-home brush as part of the treatment.

Start wherever you like on your body. Always use light, brisk strokes, moving in the direction of your heart or abdomen. Here's a sequence you can try: Brush upward from your feet to the top of your legs. Beginning at your hand, brush upward to the top of each arm then downward from your neck to the top of your abdomen. To brush your abdomen, stroke in circular motions, moving in a clockwise direction.

Spend about fifteen minutes brushing your entire body. When your skin has a pink or red tone, it's a sign that your circulation is being stimulated. Dry brushing is also thought to stimulate the lymphatic system, one of the body's natural ways of detoxifying.

Note: Dry brushing leaves the skin sensitive, so be sure to use a lotion or oil afterward to remoisturize.

Wraps

Wraps are relaxing and cleansing body treatments that encourage perspiration. At spas, wraps usually take place in a "wet room," where body coatings can be removed more easily with a hose or shower. These body coatings, or masks, are made of any number of moisturizing, aromatic, rejuvenating substances ranging from purified mud poultices to honey and mango or other fruit mixtures, paraffin wax, aloe gel or even seaweed. After the substance is applied from your neck to your toes, you are cocooned in plastic and foil or linens, towels and blankets and left to rest for twenty to thirty minutes. Cold compresses are usually applied to your forehead so you don't become overheated. After you shower, your body is remoisturized with lotion or oil.

Unlike scrubs, wraps are difficult to do at home without a partner and even then are messy, since they require hot or cold sheets along with towels and blankets for wrapping. In addition, you'll need a warm place with a table or bed to rest while you are still wrapped.

If you decide to try a wrap at home, you'll need to purchase whatever coating you want to use from a spa or body shop. Sometimes these shops even sell "kits" with all the ingredients and coverings you need to make doing a wrap at home a little easier. Therapists at the Golden Door in Escondido, California, suggest taking a shower to raise your body temperature rather than applying heat with hot sheets, then wrapping yourself with sheets soaked in cold water mixed with an essential oil for scent.

Facials

Facials are the most common type of skin care and, in some ways, may be the most important. Because your face is always exposed to the environment, it is essential to keep it clean and protected at all times. A facial is more than just a way to cleanse, however. It softens your skin and massages away tension in your forehead, around your eyes and mouth and along your jaw, which can have a relaxing effect on your whole body. Since your face is one of the most reachable parts of your body, a facial is one of the easiest treatments to do at home.

Spa facials generally include a minimum of five steps: cleansing, exfoliating, mask, massage and rehydrating (moisturizing). You can nearly duplicate the process in your own bathroom. With the proliferation of beauty products now available everywhere, all you need is a cleanser suited to your skin type, a light exfoliant, some kind of mask and a face cream for moisturizing.

You can even make some of your own products at home. Certain fruits such as papaya are natural exfoliants when mashed. For a tightening mask, you'll need some kind of clay or claylike product. Dry milk powder mixed with lemon, honey and oatmeal makes a soothing and nourishing mask. Mashed avocadoes and bananas have natural oil, making them good for moisturizing masks. If you want to experiment, test the mixture on a small patch of your skin first to make sure you aren't sensitive to the ingredients.

Like wraps and scrubs, facials should be done no more than once a week. There are as many kinds as there are products made to do them. Experiment with as many as you like, but always test products in advance on a small patch of skin. Once you have chosen your products, follow some simple steps to ensure you give your skin the best care possible. Here are instructions for a do-it-yourself facial from the Peaks at Telluride in Colorado.

▎**Relax.** *Begin your facial by draping a warm (not hot), damp towel on your face. If you want, first sprinkle it with deeply relaxing rose oil. Leave the towel on your face until it cools (about one minute).*

▎**Cleanse.** *Warm your cleanser in your hand for a few seconds so it will feel pleasant as you use it. Use gentle, circular motions as you apply it to your face. Wipe it off with a warm, wet towel or sponge.*

▎**Exfoliate.** *Apply a gentle scrub to your face with your hands. Be sure to use a fine scrub, not something too rough for your skin. Gently remove it with tepid water.*

▎**Massage.** *Start by tapping your fingers lightly along your forehead. Gently pinch your eyebrows along the brow line and then press your fingers along the bottom of your cheekbone. Rub along your jawline in a circular motion and then press your fingers along your cheekbone from your nose to your ear. Press your fingers up and down the back of your neck and then, using a circular motion, massage your scalp from your forehead to the top of your head.*

▎**Mask.** *Gently smooth on a thin film of whatever mixture you have decided to use. If you want, place cotton pads soaked in cool water on your eyelids. Lie back and relax for at least ten minutes. Rinse the mask off with tepid water and dry your face with a warm towel. Again, you can sprinkle oil on the towel or soak it in an herbal tea. Peppermint is particularly revitalizing.*

▎**Rehydrate.** *Remoisturize your skin by smoothing on a lotion or cream.*

The Healing Power of Water

Water, the simplest and most universal medium of self-care, has been recognized throughout the ages for its healing and rejuvenative properties. Rituals linking body cleansing with mental and spiritual purification are still found in many cultures. In fact, European spas were built around the same mineral springs where ancient tribes invoked spirits and Romans built elaborate baths. Many spas still thrive at these springs today.

While hydrotherapy was originally developed in Europe as a way to treat chronic conditions, it is becoming increasingly popular at modern spas as a way to promote relaxation and rejuvenation. Instead of soaking for hours in natural springs, you'll be exposed to an elaborate array of baths or showers. The baths may be hot or cold, with massaging jets or still water. They may be scented with aromatherapy oils or filled with mineral salts, seaweed, mud imported from traditional healing spots or other soothing or relaxing ingredients. The showers may have high-powered hoses, pulsating jets or light misting sprays from an overhead sprinkler. Even if you don't have multi-jet-powered shower heads or deep soaking tubs, it isn't difficult to simulate these treatments in your own bathroom.

The benefits of water can be many. Water has a great capacity to affect your body's temperature. Warm baths and showers soothe muscles, release tension and increase circulation. The massaging effect of a shower or whirlpool promotes relaxation. The buoyancy of bath water, especially when the temperature closely matches that of your body, gives you a pleasur-able feeling of lightness and ease. For all these reasons, water is basic to maintaining an overall sense of well-being. Here are some ways to get the most from home water treatments.

A stimulating shower The simplest shower can become an invigorating water therapy just by alternating the temperature from cool to warm. This is an easy way to wake up your system and stimulate your circulation. Avoid shocking yourself with extreme temperatures, and shift gradually, not abruptly, from warm to cool. Repeat the sequence two or three times.

To get a massaging effect, you may need to invest in a shower head that allows you to control water pressure. Start by turning the pressure high, so that pulsating jets massage the tight areas in your neck and shoulders. Don't forget your head. End by turning the pressure low, so that a light, relaxing mist sprays your body just before you get out. It's a refreshing way to start the day.

A relaxing steam A steam shower or sauna in your home or local fitness club can be a stress-relieving treatment by itself. Start by spending no more than ten to twelve minutes in the heat, then cool off with a quick shower. Now spend an equal amount of time resting on a chaise or towel-covered bench with your eyes closed. For maximum benefit, repeat the heating/cooling sequence two or three times.

A rejuvenating bath To get the most from a bath, you need to make sure to reserve enough time. Twenty minutes in the water is considered optimal, though for the most relaxation and enjoyment, set aside an hour and try this traditional spa sequence:

Begin by scrubbing your body with a loofah, brush or exfoliating product in a shower.

Then recline in a warm bath for twenty minutes and towel off, making sure to keep yourself warm.

Now find a quiet, warm space to lie down and rest for twenty minutes. Place a rolled towel under your bent knees to relax your back, and close your eyes or cover them with a soft pad.

End your bath ritual by lightly massaging oils or lotion onto your body to moisturize your skin.

For baths, warm, not hot, water is most relaxing. Make sure the temperature is comfortable enough so that you can lie in the bath for twenty minutes without becoming overheated. Baths over 100 degrees may cause fatigue rather than revitalize and they also dry the skin.

Place a cool towel on your forehead during your bath, and drink plenty of water to keep from becoming overheated. If you don't have time to rest afterward, at least take a cool shower when you finish to bring your body temperature back down to normal.

Finally, feel free to follow the spa example and add herbs, oils, mud, seaweed or salts to your bath to make it more relaxing, energizing, soothing or stimulating. You can find such products in most spa boutiques and bath and beauty shops near your home or even at your local drug or grocery store. Many catalogs also offer spa-type products that add an extra dimension to your home treatment. Here are a few that can really help:

Seaweed or **mud** *products are best for soothing and rejuvenating the skin. Milk also works well. Just add up to two cups of dried milk powder to your bath and lie back and relax.*

Salts *work well for aching or overworked muscles. You can find everything on the market from Dead Sea salts to mineral salts from pools in Europe. Also effective is basic epsom salt. Add a cup or two to your bath and feel your muscles unwind.*

Aromatherapy oils and **herbal bath essences** *add the sensuous pleasure of scent and may be particularly beneficial for reducing stress. There are hundreds of oils available these days, and you'll need to experiment to discover the scents you like best. To recreate a spalike herbal bath, make "tea bags" by putting a handful of fresh or dried herbs in a tea ball or nylon stocking and letting it sit under the faucet or float while you soak.*

> ## "We need less tube time and more tub time."
> Jonathan Paul De Vierville, director, Alamo Plaza Spa

Making the Most of a Massage

Of all the body treatments available at spas, massage is the best known and most popular. But you don't have to go to a spa to enjoy this pleasurable experience. High-quality licensed massage therapists are available almost everywhere and will often come right to your home. If you can afford to do it, it's best to invest in a professional. Massage is truly about the art of touch, and although you can certainly learn to work on yourself or a partner, nothing can replace the skill of a professional.

Talk to friends or to someone at your local health club or day spa to get recommendations of qualified massage therapists. You might try several until you find the right one. When you do, communicate. Giving your therapist feedback is the best way to ensure you get the

> ### "By touching the skin, you touch the core of a person."
> Anne Bramham, founder and president, the Bramham Institute, PGA National Resort and Spa

most out of your massage. Most will ask if you want hard or light pressure, and you shouldn't be afraid to speak up during the massage if you aren't comfortable. Massage can be vigorous but shouldn't be painful or unenjoyable. You'll know you're getting a good one when it's over way before you want it to be.

Privacy is never an issue with well-trained therapists. They leave the room while you are undressing and dressing and drape sheets over your body in such a way that you never feel

The Power of Scent

Scent is a powerful mood stimulator that adds greatly to any home beauty ritual. Aromatherapy, once a term used mainly for massages given with essential oils, now tends to be used to describe all treatments and products with scintillating scents. Spas have long incorporated scents from herbs, flowers, fruits and other plants in treatments from massages to wraps and facials. The Aveda Spa Retreat in Osceola, Wisconsin, has created its entire program around botanical products and their natural scents.

Because scent is so closely associated with a sense of place, many spas use regional flowers and herbs in their treatment products. Mango, papaya and coconut are scents used in Hawaii, while sage permeates the treatment rooms in Arizona and Utah. Head to a mountain spa, and you'll likely find high-alpine wildflowers used to scent oils or creams.

Aromatherapy comes in many forms today. Fresh or dried herbs are infused in baths or placed in steam showers. Essential oils, which are distilled herb and plant essences, are used in baths or blended with a base oil and used in massages. You can create your own atmosphere with scented candles or by adding a few drops of oil to bowls of water in any room.

Plants and herbs have a variety of medicinal properties and have been used for healing, purification and cleansing throughout the centuries. At right are some of the characteristics attributed to commonly used herbs, spices and other plants. Enhance your home environment by using them alone or in various combinations to achieve a desired effect.

RELAXING/CALMING
Lavender
Rose
Geranium
Marjoram
Sandalwood
Chamomile
Lemongrass
Lemon balm
Palmaroca

UPLIFTING
Ylang-Ylang
Clary sage
Bergamot
Tangerine
Geranium
Coriander
Cypress
Grapefruit
Orange
Sage
Tea tree
Thyme

INVIGORATING/ STIMULATING
Rosemary
Mint
Ginger
Basil
Camphor
Lemon
Wintergreen
Bay
Birch
Cardamom
Nutmeg
Pine
Juniper

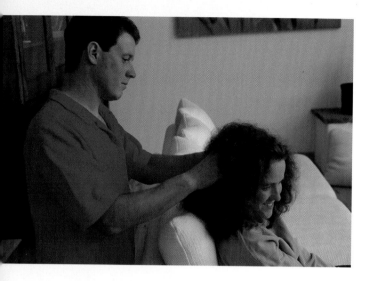

Don't forget about massages that focus specifically on your extremities. If you've never experienced reflexology (foot massage), for example, you're in for a real treat. No matter where you live, your feet, hands and head are more exposed to the elements and generally more active than other parts of your body. As a result, they are more vulnerable to fatigue and accumulated tension. Localized massage, which may be combined with facials, pedicures, manicures or hair treatments, can be powerfully relaxing for your entire body.

Home Massage

Learning to give a massage to a partner isn't difficult. It's even possible—though it may be less satisfying—to use some of these easy techniques on yourself.

When getting started, use an oil or moisturizer to make the rubbing a little smoother. You can also add a scent to a base oil such as olive, sweet almond or sesame. Always keep at least one hand on the person you are massaging to ensure you maintain a connection. Use your weight to apply pressure rather than just the strength of your hands. Above all, be sensitive to your partner's responses. A little caring touch goes a long way.

At Norwich Inn & Spa in Norwich, Connecticut, partners can practice massage techniques on each other under the watchful eye of a therapist. Here are some specifics to try on your own.

For head, neck and shoulders

▌ *Have your partner lie down, face up, with a rolled towel tucked under slightly bent knees. Stand behind your partner's head.*

exposed. You should also feel free to request a male or female therapist if you have a preference. If you still feel uncomfortable, try an Eastern-style massage in which you remain clothed, or opt for a head, neck and shoulder massage or foot massage as an alternative.

Spas offer a wide range of massages, from the classic Swedish to Japanese shiatsu to Hawaiian lomi-lomi. You'll also find specialized varieties, such as sports massage, which focuses on specific muscles that have been strained from various sports activities; lymph drainage, designed to stimulate your body's lymph system; and aromatherapy, in which essential oils are used for additional stress-relieving effects. More subtle body work includes Reiki, cranial-sacral and Polarity, which all rely on gentle movement or energy sensing rather than actual pressure. If you're confused, any therapist will be happy to explain the differences at length to help you choose the massage that sounds best. As you grow more comfortable, you may want to try experimenting with various types of massage until you come up with those you like the most.

■ *Begin by stroking your fingertips from the chin upward along the jaw line.*

■ *Rub around the joint at the top of the jaw and then around both temples.*

■ *Tap your fingertips from the middle of the forehead down to the side of the head. Then tap on both sides of the nose and along the bone running under the eyes.*

■ *Place your hands under the neck and stroke upward with the fingers of one hand while the other supports the head.*

■ *Massage into the area around the base of the skull. Then, while still supporting the head, carefully pull the head up, stretching the neck gently.*

■ *Place your thumbs at the crown of the head and make contact with your fingers on the scalp. Rub all over the scalp.*

■ *Gently massage and pull on the ears.*

■ *Place your fingertips facing each other along the breastbone, just underneath the collarbones. Stroke out to both sides.*

■ *Slide your hands under the shoulder blades and stroke upward, moving your hands to the back of the head in one long motion.*

■ *Pinch gently along the fleshy tops of both shoulders.*

■ *Gently turn your partner's head. Place your fist in the area between the neck and the right shoul-*

der blade. Roll your fist back and forth. Repeat on the left side.

For hands
■ *Have your partner sit or lie down, face up.*

■ *Hold one of your partner's hands, palm up, in both of yours. Beginning at the wrist, work your thumbs toward the fingertips.*

■ *Squeeze the fleshy part of the hand between the thumb and the forefinger between your thumb and forefinger.*

■ *Rub your knuckles in a circular motion into the palm of your partner's hand.*

■ *Pull up on each finger from base to tip.*

■ *Gently stretch each palm backward with both of your hands.*

> **"Your hands touch everything. They, too, need to be touched."**
> Lisa Dobloug, spa consultant and marketing director, Rémy Laure

For feet
■ *Have your partner sit or lie down, face up.*

■ *Rub each foot quickly with both hands to warm and get them used to being touched.*

■ *Take one foot in both your hands and stroke the arch with both thumbs pointing toward the ball of the foot.*

■ *Still using your thumbs, work up toward the ball of the foot.*

Hot Stone Massage

The most popular massage at Miraval Life in Balance is one using stones found in local Arizona riverbeds. The stones, with their deep, penetrating heat, act as a heating pad, stimulating circulation and breaking down tension. This is an easy massage to duplicate at home, with a partner or even on yourself. And it feels wonderful.

▍ You'll need five to ten smooth, preferably black, stones. The darker the stone, the longer it will retain heat. Try to find smooth stones that fit in the palm of your hand and that won't scratch when rubbed along your skin.

▍ Begin by placing the stones in hot water for ten minutes. Never heat the stones in a microwave; dry heat makes them crack. The water should be hot enough (between 104 and 125 degrees) to heat the stones, but not so hot that it burns your skin. When you take the stones out, be sure you can hold them comfortably in your hand. Try not to let the stones cool for long before applying them to your body.

▍ While the stones are heating, apply oil to your arms, legs and any body parts you can reach by yourself. Rub oil along your partner's back and legs. This helps the stones slide more smoothly.

▍ While the stones are still warm, rub them one at a time along the backs and sides of your legs, up and down the inside of your arms, along the top of your shoulder blades and up your neck. With a partner, you can also work on the back area.

Alternative ways to use the stones: At Miraval Life in Balance, the stones are sometimes placed on each shoulder blade and along the length of each side of the spine as you lie face down. Just the heat from the stones, without added pressure, can release tension in these areas. If you try this technique at home, always place a towel between your skin and the stones to avoid burning. The stones can also be used to reduce swelling by freezing them and wrapping them in a sock to use as a cold press.

▍ *Press your thumbs along the inside and the outside edges of the foot.*

▍ *With thumb and fingers, squeeze along each toe from base to tip.*

▍ *Run your knuckles up and down the bottom of the foot.*

▍ *With both hands, gently flex each foot up at the ankle and then bend it down.*

▍ Creating a Spa Day

With a little ingenuity and a few spalike products, you can create your own spa day or afternoon. The following is a two- or three-hour take-home routine from the Peaks in Telluride. Use it as a foundation, and add your own touches to create the perfect spa day at home.

▍ *Begin by creating a relaxing environment in your bathroom. Pick a time when you can be alone for three hours, unplug the phone, put some flowers in the room, light scented candles and set out a tape player and towels. Prepare the room so it's pleasing the moment you step into it.*

▍ *Head outside for a forty-five-minute vigorous walk or run. Push hard enough to raise your heart rate and work up a sweat. Cool off when you return before heading to your prepped bathroom for a full-body treatment.*

▍ *Start with an exfoliation or loofah scrub in the shower. Use an exfoliation product if you have one. Otherwise, a rough washcloth will work.*

▌ *Next, wash your hair and put on a conditioner or oil to leave on under a shower cap while you go through the next steps.*

▌ *Now use a pumice to smooth and massage the rough spots on your feet. Start running a warm bath with the essential oils of your choice.*

▌ *Cleanse your face and apply a mask of your choice.*

▌ *Now dim the lights and soak in the tub for twenty minutes. If you like, you can put a cool cloth over your eyes. Lie back and rest.*

▌ *Get back in the shower to rinse off the mask. Towel off gently and remoisturize your body with your favorite lotion.*

▌ *Don a warm robe and find a warm spot to lie down for another ten minutes to cool off.*

▌ *If you can arrange it in advance, now is the time for a massage therapist to come to your house for an hour. Otherwise, use a few do-it-yourself massage techniques.*

Reality Check

Pay Some Attention to Your Body Every Day

Even when you can't devote much time to body care, there are small gestures you can make each day that will make a big difference in how you feel. Enhance the environment in which you do your daily beauty and body routines with color, sound and scent. During your morning shower, pay attention to the sensation of water on your skin instead of dwelling on the day ahead. Give yourself a renewing massage when you put lotion on your skin. These small ways of heightening your senses are daily reminders that you are worth the care.

A RESTORATIVE BREAK

It's mid-afternoon, that time of day when you may begin to feel slightly lethargic or even a little drowsy. At a spa, you've exercised for most of the morning, enjoyed a delicious lunch and had a relaxing treatment or two. Now you are looking forward to winding down the day with a yoga or meditation class or maybe just spending some quiet time alone. First, you gather for a short ten or fifteen minutes with other guests on a patio or around a pool for a snack—raw vegetables with a creamy low-fat dip, fresh fruit, cool drinks or herbal teas or even a warm broth. Whatever it is, it is healthful and nutritious, and it's arrived just in time to stave off hunger pangs. Following the methods used by spas and learning to use snacks to their best advantage is one of the surest ways of finding the eating pattern that works best for you.

Snacking at spas isn't relegated strictly to mid-afternoons, though typically that is when most people start to lose focus and need a break to restore themselves. At many spas, guests are given the opportunity to eat something every three or four hours to keep their energy and spirits high. If you are someone who loses steam or even gets cranky at various points throughout the day, you may not be eating often enough. Even if you aren't exercising as much as you would be at a spa, you're still on the run all day—working, running errands, chauffeuring kids—and you may need regular snacks to keep going. Don't wait for hunger pangs to remind you. If you do, you're more likely to reach for quick-fix junk.

Not only do snacks moderate the ups and downs in your energy level, they also provide stress release, relaxation, comfort and entertainment. You may snack when you're bored or to reward yourself for accomplishing a difficult task. You may also head to the refrigerator to comfort yourself in times of distress.

Typical snacks are high in fat or sugar and almost totally lacking in nutritional content. They may give your energy level an immediate boost, but the results won't last. Besides, common snacks—potato chips, ice cream, candy bars—are foods you can't seem to stop eating until the entire bag, box or container is empty, thus adding a huge number of calories to your daily diet. Even if a snack is labeled "low-fat," it can still be high in calories and lack the nutrients you need for a real boost.

At spas, you won't find empty-calorie snacks, but you will find lots of options that are satisfying, filling and nutritious—hot vegetable broths, creative fruit drinks and raw vegetables served with tasty, low-fat dips. You'll also find bowls piled high with fruit and pitchers of water placed strategically so you can replenish yourself throughout the day. These are two good ways to make your office or home a snack-friendly environment.

Depending on your mood, you may crave certain snacks because of their texture and taste. Spa snacks run the gamut from creamy to crunchy or chewy, and from hot to cold. There are reasons for all this variety. Creamy, smooth foods, for example, tend to be comforting, while crunchy or chewy foods help release tension. It's good to give yourself the sensuous experience your body wants, and you can do it without eating high-fat, high-calorie foods. Spa nutritionists often hand out lists of substitutions, such as low-fat yogurt or frozen bananas in place of ice cream, pretzels for potato chips and sweet plums or papaya instead of a candy bar. If you spend some time thinking about what you crave, you can start making your own list.

Noticing your moods when you suddenly desire a particular food, and even keeping track of moods in a journal, may make it easier for you to find more healthful substitutions for the foods you crave. Sometimes simply writing down what you eat, when and why will help you discover patterns in the way you like to snack.

You may reach for a snack when you need a mental time-out from whatever you're doing. Snack breaks at these times can do double duty by refueling both your energy and mental powers. Even ten or fifteen minutes is enough time to enjoy a nutritious snack and take a break from concentrating on work. When you eat while working, talking on the phone, driving or performing some other activity, you're more likely to gobble without noticing when you're full. If you can, set aside a few minutes and really pay attention to what you are eating. Eat slowly, thinking only about the food and what it is doing for your health and well-being. By paying attention to when you've had enough, you may end up eating less.

Remember, too, that snacks don't have to be entirely different from the foods you eat at mealtimes. Spa nutritionists suggest splitting meal portions, eating part at your regular mealtime and saving another part for snack-

time. In fact, they would prefer to see you eat five or six small meals during the day instead of three big ones. You'll find it easier to keep your energy on an even keel and avoid eating a lot of food at one time.

Finally, never forget that water is the ultimate snack. It is just as important for your energy and well-being as anything else you put into your body. Often when you are feeling tired and low, you may be in need of water instead of food, even if you don't feel thirsty. At work and at home, keep a bottle handy and drink it all day long.

Nourishing Snack Alternatives

It's important to remember that snacking isn't bad. In face, it plays a major role in healthful living, helping to sustain your energy, alertness and attitude throughout the afternoon. The biggest problem with the snacks many people choose is that they're lacking in nourishment and high in sugar and fat. Even many of the reduced-fat snacks selling today have lots of calories.

Instead of reaching for either high- or low-fat junk, go for snacks that satisfy your cravings and nourish your body at the same time. The guacamole at the Cooper Aerobics Center in Dallas, for example, is made with a small part of an avocado added to mashed green peas. Guests get a low-fat, delicious snack and a serving of green vegetables at the same time. At the Bonaventure Resort and Spa in Fort Lauderdale, hummus made with nutritious garbanzo beans comes without oil and still manages to retain all the flavor. Low-fat dips,

such as ginger-curry at the PGA National Resort and Spa in Palm Beach Gardens, Florida, and the yogurt-cucumber dressing at Rancho La Puerta in Baja, California, make popular afternoon snacks.

Drinks can also make refreshingly healthful snacks. The warm, vegetable-based potassium broth made at the Golden Door in Escondido, California, can be especially satisfying on a cold day. Cool, calorie-free herbal teas make a flavorful alternative to sugary sodas.

Spa snacks give your energy level a boost when you need it most, which is exactly what snacks are meant to do. Here are some favorite recipes for spa snacks that make every caloric count.

GUACAMOLE
from the Cooper Aerobics Center

$1/2$ cup canned green peas, rinsed with cool water for 2 minutes and drained

2 tablespoons low-fat mayonnaise

1 tablespoon lemon juice

$1/4$ medium avocado, peeled, pitted, and slightly mashed

$1/2$ cup chopped tomato

$1/4$ cup finely chopped onion

1 tablespoon salsa

$1/4$ teaspoon garlic salt

$1/4$ teaspoon chili powder

1. In a food processor, process peas, mayonnaise, and lemon juice until ultra-smooth.
2. Transfer to a mixing bowl. Stir in remaining ingredients.
3. Cover and chill for at least 1 hour. Adjust seasonings as desired. Serve with baked tortilla chips.
Makes 2 cups
AUTHORS' NOTE: This guacamole tastes so much like the real thing that our tasters couldn't tell the difference.

HUMMUS
from Bonaventure Resort and Spa

$2 1/2$ cups garbanzo beans, rinsed

$1 1/2$ tablespoons lemon juice

2 cloves garlic, minced

1 teaspoon cumin

$1 1/2$ tablespoons parsley

1. In a blender or food processor, blend all ingredients until mixture reaches desired consistency.

2. Chill and serve cold with whole-wheat pita wedges.

Makes 2 cups

NOTE: For a creamier texture, add ¹/₄ to ¹/₂ cup water.

CURRY-GINGER DIPPING SAUCE

from the PGA National Resort and Spa

1 cup plain low-fat yogurt

1 green onion, minced

1 tablespoon curry powder

¹/₄ teaspoon ground ginger

Pinch sugar

Salt to taste

1. In a small bowl, stir all ingredients until well blended.

2. Cover and refrigerate for at least 1 hour to blend flavors. Serve with raw vegetables.

Makes 1 cup

YOGURT-CUCUMBER DRESSING

from Rancho La Puerta

1 medium cucumber, peeled, halved lengthwise, seeded, and cut into 1-inch pieces

¹/₄ cup fresh parsley leaves, packed

1 green onion, cut in 1-inch pieces

¹/₄ cup low-fat plain yogurt or cottage cheese

2 tablespoons fresh lemon juice

1 tablespoon white wine vinegar

1 garlic clove, halved

Freshly ground black pepper

1. In food processor or blender, combine all ingredients except pepper until smooth.

2. Season with pepper to taste. Serve with raw vegetables.

Makes 1¹/₂ cups

HOT PINEAPPLE GINGER DRINK

from the ISPA Collaboration

2 cups water

1 cup fresh or canned pineapple chunks

1 orange, peeled and sectioned

2 cups unsweetened pineapple juice

2 whole cloves

1 cinnamon stick

1-inch piece fresh ginger, peeled

1. Simmer all ingredients in a large saucepan over medium-low heat for 20 to 30 minutes.

2. Strain. Serve warm.

Makes 4 cups

POTASSIUM BROTH

from the Golden Door

46 ounces (1 large bottle) V-8 juice

2 cups water

3 cups vegetable trimmings, such as celery branches, mushrooms, zucchini, onion, green onion, bell pepper, parsley stems, lettuce, and carrots

1 teaspoon chili pepper flakes (optional)

1 teaspoon dried basil

1. Place all ingredients in a large saucepan and bring to a boil. Lower heat and simmer for about 40 minutes.

2. Strain and serve hot or cold.

Makes 6 cups

Food and Your Feelings

Whatever your particular snacking habits, they didn't develop overnight or in simple response to your body's need for food. Instead of always worrying about *what* you eat, perhaps you need to think more about *why* you eat. You may be someone who snacks when you're bored, tired, happy or depressed. Nothing to do? Head for the refrigerator. A tough day at work? Ice cream will make you feel better. Can't sleep? Maybe cookies and milk will help. Everyone has such food triggers, set off by feelings and emotions and often difficult to control. Everyone's cues are different, but by taking some time to understand the emotional states that drive you to eat and the kinds of foods you crave at those times, you'll learn to eat proactively rather than reactively.

According to spa nutritionists, the feel of the food you want is the key to understanding your cravings. Do you want something chewy, bready or creamy? Does it need to be sweet and warm to satisfy you? The urge for something crunchy may be prompted by tension in your neck and jaws that needs to be released. In that case, foods that take a lot of chewing—crackers, popcorn and pretzels—will bring the greatest relief. Alternatively, you may reach for creamy foods when you need to feel soothed and nurtured. Pudding, peanut butter, cheese, milkshakes, chocolate, caramel and ice cream are comforting foods, all the more sedating when they are sweet. Warm foods, such as freshly baked bread or homemade apple pie, may also be associated with comfort and care. Those who need to feel more secure may

lean toward heavier, filling foods, such as pasta, potatoes and waffles.

These cravings are a sign of emotional or sensual needs, so it makes sense that you may overdose on the foods that give you the greatest satisfaction at the moment. Whatever they are, your needs are real, and depriving yourself of foods that can help meet these needs isn't necessarily the right solution. There are, however, some simple snacks suggested by nutritionists at spas that have the same emotionally satisfying tastes and textures as traditional snacks, but with less fat and calories:

Bready Snacks

Low-fat bran muffin

Baked potato

Baked acorn squash

Angelfood cake

Crunchy Snacks

Plain, oven-dried bagel chips

Air-blown popcorn

Unsalted whole-grain pretzels

Baked tortilla chips

Animal crackers

Sweetened cereals

Rice cakes

Sweet Snacks

Baked apples

Baked sweet potato

Grapes (frozen, they taste like sherbet)

Fruit sorbet

Popsicles

Plums

Frozen yogurt

Creamy Snacks

Yogurt

Ricotta cheese

Part-skim mozzarella cheese

Frozen bananas

Smoothies

Chewy Snacks

Bagels

Dried fruit

Tootsie rolls

Gumdrops

Warm Snacks

Clear consommé

Oatmeal

Steamed vegetables

Potassium broth

Heated vegetable juices

Changing Stubborn Snack Habits

Sometimes substituting healthful foods when you crave a snack isn't possible, especially when the triggers are very strong and your environment is practically demanding that you eat. You may think it's impossible to sit through a movie without buttery popcorn and consequently, after buying your ticket, head for the refreshment counter without even thinking about it. Sporting events are other big snack triggers. With vendors throwing hot dogs and peanuts into the crowd, it can be difficult to sit snackless through a baseball or football game. Other cues may be more subtle, but just as powerful. Perhaps there's an irresistible cookie emporium near your workplace. Maybe your boss likes to pass out doughnuts at afternoon meetings. Even the crinkling sound of a potato chip bag or the sight of an open box of cookies when you first get home from work can be a trigger to begin eating.

Understanding how your environment prompts you to eat is the first step toward changing your habits. At Green Mountain at Fox Run in Ludlow, Vermont, for example, guests are taught that most people have only two or three high-risk situations in which they are likely to overeat. Once you identify what those are for you, it's easier to make a plan for coping with them in advance. It's really a question of applying the same planning skills you use to organize your work and family life to an eating habit you want to change. Eventually you'll find ways to get the results you want.

To get you started, Canyon Ranch in Tucson suggests these strategies for helping you break or change stubborn snack habits.

▍ *Put some distance between yourself and the food you want to resist. Don't keep cookies in the house. Move away from the places and situations that trigger you to eat. If you pass by your favorite ice cream shop on your way home from work each day, take another route or walk on the opposite side of the street. You'll have more luck resisting cravings if the food isn't right in front of you.*

▍ *If possible, temporarily avoid social situations, people or events that influence you to eat too much or trigger strong "must-eat" emotions. Forgo that baseball game or movie until you feel you can handle it without loading up on junk food. When you feel strong enough or have figured out alternatives, you can resume those activities.*

▍ *If there's a snack you simply can't give up, don't. It's obviously meeting a need. If chocolate is your passion, don't fight it, but eat only one truffle instead of ten. By savoring the small amount you allow yourself and not feeling guilty, you may find you don't want any more. You can also help yourself by buying individual portions or small packages instead of family- or economy-sized portions.*

Creating a Snack-Friendly Environment

Your snack habits will improve immediately if you turn your home or office into a snack-friendly environment. Begin by making sure the snack foods around you have lots of nutritional value and are stocked in abundance during those hours when you traditionally want to eat between meals.

According to nutritionists at the Cooper Aerobics Center in Dallas, a refrigerator and a blender are the most important aids in creating a healthful snack environment. If you can keep skim milk or yogurt on hand, even in the workplace, you have a ready snack packed with protein and nutrients, particularly when the milk or yogurt is paired with cereal. Another excellent snack is a strawberry and banana smoothie blended with skim milk. If you freeze the fruit, you won't even need to add ice. With a blender in your office or kitchen, it takes only a couple of minutes to put together this milkshake-like snack that is a real energy booster.

The most important thing to remember is to fill up on nutritional snacks, not empty calories. Cookies may be delicious, but with little or no nutritional value, they're really a dessert, not a snack. Here are some additional tips from the nutritionist at the Cooper Aerobics Center for ways to get and keep your environment snack-friendly.

▍ *Keep bowls of whole fruit handy in your kitchen or office. Make sure the fruit is changed twice each week so that it always looks and tastes enticing.*

If you like to sip on something warm during the day, keep a basket of herbal tea bags on the counter near a pot of hot water instead of brewing coffee. One cup of coffee in the morning is fine. But if you are a chronic coffee drinker who needs caffeine to get an energy boost, take a closer look at other, more nutritional ways to get that lift you need. You may need to get more sleep at night or to eat more at breakfast or lunch.

Warmed juices and broths can be very filling. If you have a microwave handy, try warming up some V-8 juice during your next snack break. It's as delicious as tomato soup and very low in calories.

Carrot sticks are the most convenient way to get more vegetables into your diet. They require no utensils and are easy to store bagged and prepeeled. Best of all, they're a naturally sweet snack that can be eaten throughout the day.

If you like bready snacks, try stocking your office or kitchen pantry with rice cakes. They have no fat and are very low in calories. You'll also get more for your snack, since an entire bag of rice cakes has about the same number of calories as a bagel.

Make a rule at your office to bring only healthful items into communal areas. If someone wants to share chocolate chip cookies, ask him or her to keep them in a private area. It's easier to put coffee cake or pizza out of mind if it's out of sight.

Always remember to drink water throughout the day. At the office, keep cups with flat instead of pointed bottoms near the water cooler so you can take water back to your desk.

When Food Fills Your Time

At spas, it's not unusual for guests to forget altogether about snacking between meals. Not only are spa guests well fed at meal times, they are also busy all day long, engaged with others, trying new activities and even rediscovering some they used to enjoy. They don't need to reach for food to fill their time.

If food is the first thing you think of to alleviate boredom, loneliness or stress, you may need to start looking for other ways to get pleasure and play back into your life. At Canyon Ranch, guests seeking help with eating issues are encouraged to look into their past for clues to what is missing in their lives. It's a technique anyone can try. If you liked to paint as a child but haven't picked up a brush for years, why not give it another try? If you love books but never seem to have much time for reading, try listening to books on tape as you drive or do household chores. If you love the outdoors, consider starting a garden. Take up the piano or learn to make quilts or pottery.

> **"By default, eating is often the only game we play."**
>
> Julie Waltz Kembel, education director, Health and Healing Center, Canyon Ranch

Many people use eating as a way to get in touch with their bodies, particularly if their work is intellectual rather than physical, or if their lives are sedentary in general. If this sounds like you, try revitalizing your senses by taking long, leisurely outdoor walks, warm, scented baths or regular massages. If isolation is driving you to eat and you find yourself turning to food as a substitute for a best friend, seek out activi-

ties that will connect you to others. Sign up for a dance class, join a reading group or try out for a community play. The idea is not to distract yourself from eating but to find more pleasurable, positive ways to fill the voids in your life.

▮ Tracking Your Eating Patterns

If most of your food cravings seem to surface between meals, you may need to sort out what's driving this pattern before you can

begin to change your snacking habits. Keeping a food journal can help you do that, and many spa nutritionists recommend it. Just by making the commitment to record what you eat, you will start to become conscious of your eating habits as you never were before. Developing such awareness is invaluable, especially if you've always felt at the mercy of food cravings.

As with other kinds of journals, there is no one right way to keep a food journal. Yours should reflect those things about yourself you want to discover, eventually revealing patterns and connections that can help you make changes. You might want to start by simply recording what you eat, when you eat and why, taking note of your energy levels and moods at the time. Be as honest as you can. No one is looking at your journal but you, and its purpose is to aid, not judge.

Look for patterns to emerge. When are your energy levels highest and lowest? When do you eat too much or too little? Do you feel guilty when you snack? What foods do you crave? Are there certain situations that trigger you to snack? A journal will help put the answers to all these questions right in front of you. After noticing particular patterns, you can use your journal to make changes, set goals and record results.

The thought of recording your food habits may seem overwhelming at first, but it really isn't. As with any part of your life in which you are trying to make changes, problems often loom larger in your imagination than in reality, and once you focus on your particular concerns, the answers are likely to be simpler than you thought. Maybe the news won't be all bad. Maybe you aren't really the binge eater you thought you were but only someone who wants ice cream every time you watch a late-night movie. Perhaps you'll find that an apple and a small piece of cheese at three o'clock in the afternoon are all you need to get through the rest of the day alert and enthusiastic. You may even exorcise a lot of guilt by discovering all the healthful foods you *are* eating.

If you're trying to lose weight, you may need to get very precise about how much you are eating. Take note also of the amount of exercise you are getting to gain an accurate picture of calories taken in versus calories burned. If you are worried about not getting enough fruits and vegetables, use your journal to note the number of servings of nutritious foods you get each day. Before long you may discover that keeping a journal is an excellent way to discover your "personal best" relationship with food.

Water: The Ultimate Snack

Spas may no longer be built around springs, but water is still at the heart of their renewing powers. It's everywhere—in beauty treatments, hot tubs, baths, fountains, streams and pools. At spas, you cleanse with water, relax in water and calm your mind with the sights and sounds of water.

Most important of all, you drink water. At spas, pitchers of water are placed in exercise studios, in rest areas, in dining rooms and in bedrooms. Guests are encouraged to drink water when they wake, when they exercise, when they eat and when they play. If you aren't in the habit of drinking lots of water already, by the time you leave a spa, you will be.

Water is the source of life itself. It needs to be flowing through you all the time, like a replenishing river. Without water, your energy wanes and your spirits flag. Don't worry about drinking too much. Spa nutritionists recommend that you drink a minimum of six eight-ounce glasses of water every day. You'll need even more when you exercise or when temperatures rise. Often a glass of water is all you need to revive your energy level. Try it before you snack. It will help you feel less hungry and, in fact, may be all you really want. Reach for water whenever you exercise, work

or relax at home. Make it a regular part of your daily routine by keeping a bottle in your car, on your desk and in your refrigerator so it's never far from reach. Whenever you take a break, automatically reach for a sip of water. It's fat-free, calorie-free and freely available. It's the ultimate snack, and drinking plenty of it is the most healthful habit you can ever adopt.

Reality Check

Take a Break for Balance

Important for providing energy between meals, snacks also provide a much-needed break for your body, mind and spirit. Every hour throughout the day, make it a habit to check in with yourself. You don't always need to eat something, but you may need a break. If you've been sitting for a long period, get up, walk around and stretch. Instead of waiting until after work or the weekend to give yourself a rest, add balance to your life by taking time-outs throughout each day.

TAPPING YOUR INNER RESOURCES

It's late afternoon, that quiet time before dinner, when exercise and body treatments have worked their magic. At spas, this is the time for rest, relaxation and reflection. Some of the choices you have now mirror those of the morning, except that the yoga, stretching or t'ai chi that helped you shake off sleep upon rising will now help you slow down and turn inward. At many spas, you'll learn to calm and focus your mind by practicing any number of relaxation and meditation techniques. You might even explore your creativity through writing or painting, now that you're free of the usual distractions of life. Or you may do nothing more than lie in a hammock or sit by a waterfall, letting your mind wander. Whatever you choose, this time for reflection may lead you to your most profound discoveries. If you're not used to slowing down, you'll be amazed at what a difference it can make in your life.

Spa experts today say their guests have made great strides toward understanding the importance of diet and exercise for overall health. Now, they say, more attention needs to be given to the role of rest and relaxation. Just as regular exercise will keep your body in shape, regular relaxation will maintain your energy and joie de vivre. As complaints of fatigue, exhaustion and feelings of being overwhelmed—all side effects of chronic stress—hit what seems to be an all-time high, it is more crucial than ever for people to learn ways to combat stress before the symptoms pile up.

If you regularly experience tense muscles, a rapid pulse, racing thoughts, irritation, anxiety and a feeling of disconnectedness from others, you, like millions of others, are stressed out. By learning more about how you react to stress and ways you can help yourself to relax, you can learn to cope with stress before it interferes with the pleasure you take in living.

Typical end-of-the-day spa classes, with names like "Stretch and Relax" or "Inner Journey," are designed to teach you how to ease stress. In them, you learn techniques for releasing muscle tension, slowing breathing and heart rate and calming the mind. All are aimed at helping you discover how your mind and body constantly influence each other.

Because spas offer safe, naturally relaxing environments, explorations into areas that may be new to you are easy and comfortable. With like-minded companions to share the experience, trying self-hypnosis, meditation, visualization or restorative yoga becomes an exciting opportunity to add an extra dimension to your life. At some spas, you'll even explore ways developed by other cultures to focus inward. At Green Valley Spa and Tennis Resort in St. George, Utah, for example, you might make a medicine wheel in the Native American tradition, while at Rancho La Puerta in Baja, California, you can try drumming. The flowing Chinese martial art t'ai chi and various styles of yoga are commonly found at spas.

Whatever method you try, from simple contemplation to something more exotic, your body and mind will begin to slow together. You'll start to feel as if time itself is slowing

down and you'll be better able to live in the present, devoting your attention to what is happening at the moment. In this receptive state, you may begin to see life more clearly and notice the beauty around you in a way you hadn't before. You may even find your creativity flowing freely in poetry or art workshops. If you can learn to recall this state of mind at home, you'll be well on your way to living each day with a greater sense of well-being.

Even without the benefit of a spa or trained instructors, you can create a relaxation program using do-it-at-home techniques. Simply taking a time-out in a quiet place is the best way to begin. Though the transition time between day and evening seems like the most natural time for a break, it really doesn't matter if the time

you choose is morning, noon or night. The time that works for you is the right time. It doesn't have to be a long time, either. Setting aside fifteen or twenty minutes to slow your thoughts, stretch your body and refocus your mind can have a profound effect on the rest of your day or evening. Once the members of your family figure out how much peace those few minutes can bring, they will be more apt to let you have them without interruption.

The right environment can help slow your pace even more. If you haven't been outside all day, nature may help restore your peace of mind. Many spas have beautiful natural environments that induce relaxation the minute you step onto the grounds. Miraval Life in Balance, in the middle of the Arizona desert, is a meditative oasis with fountains and pools. At the Golden Door in Escondido, California, Japanese-style gardens create a reflective atmosphere, while at Rancho La Puerta in Baja, California, a landscape of colorful flowers is a restorative experience for the senses.

Wherever you live, the sight of the ocean, mountains, open fields, trees or gardens—or even just the sound of water trickling in a stream or flowing in a fountain—may be all it takes to restore a clearer perspective. When you've gotten caught up in the small details of your life, nature has a way of reminding you of the bigger picture.

For everyone living in our contemporary world, just getting a new perspective on daily pressures is one of the best ways to combat relentless stress. By taking a daily time-out to relax and remembering to slow down and catch your breath whenever possible, you can begin to develop a more positive outlook on each day. With time and practice, as your breath, mind and heart grow calm together, inner peace begins to become a reality. Then, you can really start to enjoy life's journey.

Relaxation: The Body-Mind Connection

Frayed nerves, forgotten details and tight muscles are all signs of stress, and nearly everyone suffers from these symptoms and more. At spas, afternoon relaxation classes, which might be anything from yoga to meditation, are aimed at teaching you ways to deal with your response to stress. Many of these classes combine a variety of elements to achieve the best results. A stretch class, for example, might include mental concentration techniques, such as a body scan or visualization, along with physical exercises to release muscle tension.

However they are mixed, all these techniques can be powerful tools for relaxing the body and mind. At home, you'll have to experiment to see which methods or combinations work best for you. Some are body-oriented techniques, while others are more cerebral; all affect you both physically and mentally. Some approaches may appeal more than others, depending on your temperament or mood. All may elicit certain physical sensations—of heaviness or lightness, tingling or warmth. Let these sensations happen without fighting them. Nothing to worry about, they are just signs that you are beginning to let go and relax. As you try each of these techniques, you'll begin to understand more clearly what they're about and how they can work for you.

> **"Freeing the mind relaxes the body. Relaxing the body frees the mind."**
> Phyllis Pilgrim, fitness director, Rancho La Puerta

It's ideal if you can set aside fifteen to twenty minutes a day to practice these relaxation exercises—in the morning before breakfast, in the late afternoon before dinner or just before bed, unless you are too tired to concentrate. Because you are *training* your body and mind to relax, you will get the best results if you practice faithfully. You are developing a skill just like any other, and it may take time before you can readily identify the state of relaxation and easily achieve the desired effects. The rewards in terms of renewed vitality and a fresh outlook on life are worth it.

Simple Relaxation

This technique, recommended by staff at Canyon Ranch in Tucson, is wonderful in part because it is so simple. It is made up of the four basic elements that are common to most methods of relaxation.

▪ **Find a quiet environment.** *Choose a calm place that's as sound-free as possible—an unoccupied office where you work or a quiet spot in your home where you won't be interrupted.*

▪ **Find a comfortable position.** *Keep muscular effort to a minimum. At spas, you'll often learn relaxation techniques in a reclining position, but many of them can be done seated as well. Either way, make sure your head and arms are supported. Loosen all tight-fitting clothing. Close your eyes.*

▪ **Use a mental device.** *The constant stimulus of repeating a single-syllable sound or word silently or in a low tone helps promote relaxation by focusing your mind. You may want to use simple, positive, affirming words, such as* calm, free *or* relaxed. *An alternative to word repetition is to count your breaths repeatedly from one to ten.*

▪ **Maintain a passive attitude.** *To really rest and let go of tension, you need a receptive frame of mind. When distracting thoughts enter your mind, let them come and then let them go. It is important not to judge yourself or scrutinize your performance, or to try to force relaxation to occur.*

Progressive Relaxation

Everyone experiences and responds to stress differently. If your muscles get very tense or you begin to feel out of touch with your body when you're under a lot of stress, this technique may work especially well for you. It involves tensing and then relaxing all of the muscles in your body, beginning with your feet and ending with your face.

▪ *Begin by lying on a comfortable surface, such as a carpet or mat.*

▪ *Inhale and squeeze your right foot and leg as tightly as possible, until your leg lifts slightly off the mat. Exhale and let your leg go.*

▪ *Take a full breath to rest, inhaling and exhaling completely.*

▪ *Repeat the process with your left foot and leg.*

▪ *Take another full-breath rest.*

▪ *Repeat the process, first by tightening and releasing the buttocks, then by pushing out and releasing the abdomen, expanding and releasing the rib cage and chest, tightening the right hand and arm, then the left, and ending by tightening all the muscles in your face before you let it relax.*

Body Scan

Sometimes performed after progressive relaxation, the body scan uses mental focus rather than muscular activity to relax various parts of the body.

▪ *Lie on your back in a comfortable position.*

▪ *Begin by focusing your mind on your right foot. Notice any sensations in the foot. Notice any images that come to mind as you concentrate. Don't judge the feelings or try to manipulate them. Just notice. If your mind wanders, gently bring your attention back to your foot.*

▌ *Continue to concentrate for a few breaths and, on an exhale, try to picture your breath passing through your foot as it leaves your body.*

▌ *Repeat the process with your left foot, right leg, left leg, pelvic area, rib cage, right arm, left arm, shoulders, neck, head and face.*

Meditation

Meditation techniques are numerous and varied, but they are all basically ways to focus and calm your mind. Frequent meditation can also help make you aware of how your typical thought patterns contribute to your stress level. The premise is very simple. Focus your attention on something like your breathing or a single-syllable word repeated over and over. If your mind starts to wander, gently bring your attention back to the focus. Don't worry that you are doing something wrong because your mind is restless. In fact, it may not be until you become quiet that you realize how much static is in your mind. Everyone has distracting thoughts; stopping or controlling them isn't necessary. Just making the repeated effort to let go of your thoughts and return to your focus is all you need to do. Here are two basic meditation practices taught by spas:

1. *Sit comfortably but erect. Close your eyes and bring your attention to your breathing. Exhale and silently count one. On the next exhale, count two. Continue through four, and begin counting again from one. If you lose track or become distracted, notice the distraction and let it go. Then start counting again from one.*

2. *Sit comfortably but erect. Close your eyes and focus your attention on your abdomen, feeling it rise as you inhale and fall as you exhale. Whenever you notice that your mind has wandered from your breathing, observe what it was that took it away, then refocus your attention on your abdomen and begin again.*

Visualization

This technique is sometimes used as a mental device after your body is already relaxed from progressive relaxation or a body scan. Because your nervous system responds to your imagination as well as to reality, sometimes just imagining beautiful places or having pleasant fantasies can lower your stress level. It may help to have a teacher or a tape that can talk you through, but you can create positive images on your own as well. The key is to touch all your senses. Here are some tips:

▌ *Lie down or seat yourself in a comfortable position.*

▌ *Imagine yourself in a favorite environment: a green forest, a beach, a mountaintop.*

▌ *Pay attention to the sights, sounds and scents of that environment. See the colors of the sky, feel the sand under your feet or the breeze on your skin. Hear the wind in the branches and smell the air. The more detail you put into the scene, the more effective your visualization will be.*

Affirmation

The process of affirmation is similar to visualization, except you use positive words instead of pictures. As with visualization, it's more effective if you've taken time to relax before you begin. The key to this technique is to phrase your suggestion to yourself as though it were already a reality. In other words, don't say to yourself, "I want to lose ten pounds." Instead, say, "I am slim and my clothes fit me well." Of course, this won't magically change anything, but by affirming or making positive suggestions to yourself, you slowly start to change your self-perception. That can be as important to achieving goals as taking the practical steps to reach them.

Self-Hypnosis

By relaxing your body and then using visualization or affirmation, you are actually engaging in self-hypnosis. There's nothing mystical about this technique. Hypnosis is really just a way of taking advantage of your relaxed, receptive mind to "input" positive suggestions. You are fully aware and in control at all times.

It isn't difficult to try hypnosis on yourself. Here are three self-hypnosis procedures offered by spas that work well for beginners. They have similarities and differences in both approach and purpose. Try them all to discover the one that works best for you.

Three-minute rapid relaxer from the Doral Golf Resort and Spa

■ *Sit in a comfortable chair in a dimly lit room. Remove your shoes, jewelry and glasses.*

■ *Maintain your present rate of respiration and think only of your breathing. Bring your attention to the inside of your nostrils and become aware of the sensation of the air being inhaled and exhaled.*

■ *Silently repeat the following chant about six to ten times: "With each breath in, my body relaxes, and with each breath out, my mind relaxes."*

■ *Keep your eyes closed and visualize a small white feather silently drifting and floating in the wind—not bound by space, time or gravity. Visualize the feather floating through the clouds and into the cool, blue sky. Silently say to yourself, "The higher it floats, the better I feel. The higher it floats, the quicker I heal." Repeat this phrase six to ten times.*

As the feather continues on its journey into infinity, your level of stress and anxiety will diminish substantially. When it floats out of your mental field of perception, you will feel serene and relaxed. At this point, slowly open your eyes.

Ten-minute relaxation and affirmation from the Golden Door

■ *Find a quiet place to sit comfortably for about ten minutes.*

■ *Close your eyes and breathe slowly and deeply for a few breaths. Think to yourself, "I am relaxing. All outside noises help me to relax more."*

■ *Relax your body sequentially from your feet to the top of your head. Think to yourself, "My feet are relaxing. My lower legs are relaxing," etc. Take your time, and let the feeling of relaxation move throughout your body. If your mind* wanders, bring your attention back to the relaxation process as soon as you realize your thoughts have drifted.

▌ When you feel relaxed, take a few minutes to focus your attention on what it is you would like to accomplish. It is important to focus on what you want, rather than on what you do not want. Think statements like "I am relaxed," instead of "I am not nervous." You may want to use a list of five or six positive suggestions to guide your imagination. Here are some examples:

▶ My body is fit and healthy.
▶ I am an excellent tennis player.
▶ I enjoy only healthful, nutritious food in the proper amount for my ideal weight.
▶ I sleep soundly every night and awaken at _____ o'clock in the morning feeling refreshed.
▶ I relax quickly and easily.
▶ My memory is better than ever.

As you think your suggestion to yourself, take a few seconds to imagine it as if it were already true. Include a sense of pride or accomplishment to reinforce it. Make your suggestion as real in your mind as possible. If your mind shifts into negative thoughts, simply reinforce the positive.

▌ After approximately ten minutes, complete your session, either by drifting off to sleep if you are practicing at bedtime or by reenergizing yourself by breathing deeply, moving and stretching.

▌ Repeat this process daily for best results. As you accomplish your goals, you may replace the statements with new ones.

Fifteen-minute meditation and suggestion from the Greenhouse

▌ Find a quiet place where you can be alone. Sit in a chair or on the floor and just be silent. See how still you can become.

▌ Begin to notice any sounds in the room: the clock, the air conditioner, the ceiling fan.

▌ After you become comfortable with the sounds in the room, begin noticing any physical sensations. Just notice them and let your mind move on.

▌ Begin observing your thoughts. Let them rise like bubbles to the surface, pop and disappear.

▌ When you are ready, make a positive suggestion to yourself, such as "I am comfortable in social situations." Use only one suggestion at each session.

> **"Meditation simply means turning down the static so you can hear what's going on internally."**
> Dr. John Painter, director, Mind-Body Programs, The Greenhouse

Make sure you phrase it in the present tense. Say, "I am," not, "I would like to be."

▌ *Attach a visual image to your suggestion. Make it realistic. To attain it, you must be able to imagine it.*

▌ *After your session, forget about your suggestion for the rest of the day. Give this process time to work by repeating it every day for at least thirty days.*

▌ The Many Faces of Yoga

Yoga is not only a great fitness builder but an equally good relaxation method that integrates mind and body. Many people find it is the only way they can become centered after a busy day, and claim it has made a huge difference in their lives. Increasingly popular, yoga is taught in spas and gyms across the country. You may find Iyengar, Astanga or some other type of hatha, or physical, yoga. With its hundreds of different postures, yoga builds strength, endurance and energy, and promotes flexibility, mental receptivity and relaxation. Classes offered at the end of the day at spas tend to emphasize calming postures, along with deep breathing, to help guests wind down.

By integrating mental focus and breathing with exercises that stretch and strengthen your whole body, yoga is an unsurpassed way to develop greater body awareness and self-confidence, as well as an effective way to relax.

Some emphasize strength and endurance, others promote flexibility and relaxation and

many develop all of these elements of fitness at once. It is this all-in-one approach that converts people into yoga enthusiasts. By using your whole body in an integrated way, you discover your body's imbalances and start to correct them. Better posture, better breathing and the elimination of chronic aches and pains are common results.

If you want to get involved in yoga, it's best to try a variety of classes so you can see what style of yoga you like best. Your teacher is important as well, since yoga postures need to be taught with sensitivity. Your body will be in unaccustomed positions that can be risky if you are not ready for them, and your teacher must be sure you are adequately prepared. Yoga should never be painful. Good teachers give you more challenging postures, such as backbends or handstands, only when you are ready to try them. In good hands, yoga can be exhilarating and a wonderful way to relieve stress.

Restorative Yoga for Deep Rest

Restorative yoga is a specialized form of yoga practice that focuses on slowing down the body and mind to provide much-needed rest and renewal. Restorative yoga differs from other varieties primarily because its postures are all completely passive. You might do something as simple as lie on the floor. Or you might sit or lie propped with bolsters or blankets to support your head, back, legs and arms. The idea is to position yourself so that you use the least amount of muscular effort possible and leave your body virtually strain-free. Very soon, tight muscles release

and your mind begins to relax.

The postures involved in restorative yoga are not hard to learn, but the positioning and use of props is very important, so you may want to learn from an expert in the beginning. To get a taste, you can try two simple postures taught at the Claremont Resort and Spa in Berkeley, California, and at Rancho La Puerta.

They can be performed on a bare floor, but a carpet, mat or even grassy area outside will be more comfortable. If you do both postures in one session, do them in the order given here for five to ten minutes each. If you want to do just one, skip the first and try the second for a period of five to twenty minutes for the best effect.

Legs-Up-on-the-Wall Posture If you've been traveling or on your feet all day, this is wonderful for draining tension out of your legs.

▌ *Lie down with your legs against a bare wall. Put a folded blanket, an inch or two thick, under your head and neck to keep your head from dropping back. To get into position, sit sideways to the wall with your shoulder nearly touching it and swing your legs up the wall as you roll onto your back.*

▌ *If your buttocks and lower back are lifting off the floor at all, you need to move away from the wall slightly. You should feel comfortable and supported, particularly in your neck and lower back. Keep your legs straight but relaxed and your arms slightly out from your sides, palms up.*

▌ *Close your eyes and take a few deep breaths. Try to imagine all the tension draining out of your legs.*

▌ *Stay in this position for five to ten minutes. Then open your eyes and take a few breaths. Roll to one side and take a few more breaths before slowly pushing yourself up into a seated position.*

Basic Relaxation Posture This is a great refresher when you are feeling particularly drained or tired.

▌ *Fold one blanket an inch or two thick to put under your head and neck, and fold another into a square and then roll it up.*

▌ *Lie down. Place your head and neck on the folded blanket and put the rolled one under your slightly bent knees. Let your arms rest away from your sides, with your palms up. Close your eyes. Be sure you feel comfortable, then just relax.*

▌ *Now take a few long, deep breaths, then breathe normally. Notice where your body is holding tension and imagine it releasing from those areas. Repeat this pattern, continuing to release any tension as you feel it.*

▌ *You may remain in this pose for five to twenty minutes. When you are ready, open your eyes, take a few deep breaths, then roll to your side and slowly sit up.*

▌ Taking a Breather

Breathing is central to every mind-body technique from meditation to martial arts. Its rhythm underlies the smooth movements you make in t'ai chi and helps you sustain the postures in yoga. Breathing is also central to such mind-calming spiritual practices as chanting and singing.

Breathing is natural, something you do most of the time without a thought. Yet, by focusing on it or making an effort to alter its speed and depth, it becomes the most accessible link you have to your body and mind, one that can be called upon to help calm you down at any time of the day or night.

On some occasions it isn't necessary to control your breathing for it to have a calming effect. In meditation, for example, you move into a relaxed state by using your breath as a focal point. In this case, simply paying attention to your breathing, without making any effort to change it, can give you pause and perspective, even during very stressful situations.

Your breathing is also a good barometer of your emotional condition. When you are experiencing stress, for example, your breath becomes shallow and quick, an instinctive reaction to real or imaginary threat. If you are stressed on an ongoing basis, you may find yourself regularly short of breath, which will make you feel tired and tense. Changing your pattern of breathing can have a powerful effect. By concentrating on slowing and deepening your breath, you send a message to your nervous system that it's time to calm down. At the same time, you augment your oxygen supply and ease tension and fatigue.

The key is the exhale. Slow and deepen your breath by exhaling all your air through your mouth, pressing in your abdomen to empty your lungs more fully. Then breathe in as deeply as you can, allowing your abdomen to fill like a balloon. Doing this a couple of times is often enough to break a stressful breathing cycle and release some tension from your body.

Some simple breathing exercises will help you learn to listen more closely to your body and equip you with another method for natural relaxation. These techniques, from Miraval Life in Balance, Canyon Ranch and Rancho La Puerta, take only a few minutes and can be done whenever you need a breather during the day.

Mindful Breathing

▮ *Sit or lie comfortably with your eyes closed and focus all your attention on your abdomen. Feel it rise, or expand, gently as you inhale and fall, or recede, as you exhale.*

▮ *Keep your attention focused and stay with the full breath, as if you were riding the rhythm of your own breathing.*

▮ *Go through one or two complete breaths, or more if you wish.*

▮ *Be aware of your thoughts and feelings as you breathe, observing them without judging them or yourself. At the same time, try to be aware of any changes in the way you are seeing things and feeling about yourself.*

▮ *Open your eyes and continue with your day.*

A Relaxing Break

▮ *Sit in a comfortable position with your eyes closed and pay attention to your breathing.*

▮ *Think only about your breath as it flows in and out of your body.*

▮ *Say something to yourself such as: "I am relaxing, breathing smoothly and rhythmically. Fresh oxygen flows in and out of my body. I feel calm, renewed and refreshed."*

▮ *Continue thinking only about the smooth, rhythmical process of your breathing.*

▮ *After five minutes, open your eyes, stand up, stretch and continue with your daily activities.*

Deepening Your Breath

▮ *Lie down with your eyes closed. Begin by exhaling fully through your mouth.*

Now begin to inhale, first filling your abdomen, then your rib cage and then your upper chest. As you exhale, reverse the order, first emptying your upper chest, then your rib cage and finally flattening your abdomen.

Notice where your breathing is easy and where it is difficult—where you can feel movement as the air moves in and where it feels stiff. Let the stiff areas yield without using strain or force.

Continue to breathe for four or five full cycles.

Open your eyes, roll over to a sitting position and rise slowly. Before you return to your activities, notice if and how you feel different.

Slowing Down Your Day

Whatever results you expect from a spa visit, what may strike you is the way time seems to slow down. Though you are busy from dawn to dusk, the combination of exercise, relaxing treatments, inner reflection and attention to yourself is usually so restorative that the sense of urgency that usually fills your days disappears completely. Within a few days you are moving more slowly, breathing more deeply and beginning to notice your surroundings instead of constantly thinking about the past or the future. This sense of timelessness is sometimes called "being in the present," and it's the best possible antidote to constant worry about not having enough time.

Of course, it's easy to attain this "living in the moment" state at a spa, away from family and business pressures and with no one to

Finding a Quiet Time

Telephones, television, loud music, computer games, barking dogs and shouting kids may seem to conspire to keep you from finding some quiet time at home each day to relax. Forget ten or fifteen minutes—even a few moments of silence may seem precious. Unfortunately, there's no easy answer. If you wait for a quiet time to materialize, chances are it never will. You have to find it for yourself.

One idea, taken from Skylonda Fitness Retreat in Woodside, California, is to implement a quiet hour. At this spa, a no-talking rule goes into effect each day from five to six o'clock. Guests may take meditation or yoga classes, nap, write postcards or stroll the grounds. But they must do it in silence.

Perhaps an hour a day of "quiet time" at your house is a far-fetched idea. In that case, how about an hour once or twice a week? Or even half an hour a day. Make it a fun time for the kids by creating a game. Ask them to see how long they can go without making any noise. Or implement a "reading hour" for them during your quiet time.

If that still doesn't work, you may need to physically remove yourself from your home and find another place where you can be quiet. Pick a place that is not only quiet but makes you feel good. At a spa, you might sit in a garden or by a fountain, or lie in a hammock under a tree. At home, you may find that just getting out into nature is all it takes to make you feel centered and relaxed. A simple walk in fresh air amid pretty scenery can be restorative by itself. Finding outdoor beauty is easy if you live in the mountains, near a forest or by a large park. If not, you may have to improvise. Find a stream or a private garden where you can sit quietly and reflect, or search out parks with fountains, pools or waterfalls.

Once you have found a quiet time and place, immerse yourself in your surroundings and let yourself be nurtured by the calmness of the moment. Silence alone can be restful and healing.

think of but yourself. As soon as you return home, you may feel yourself being pulled in so many directions again that it's hard to think of anything except how you are going to find more time.

If you take the time to do them on a regular basis, any of the relaxation techniques described in this chapter will help. Even though you may still be as busy as ever, you can train yourself to feel less panicked about time by learning to be less reactive, even under the most stressful circumstances.

Spa experts also recommend some very simple steps you can take to maintain a state of calm. If you remind yourself to do them until they become second nature, you will find that they make more of a difference than you ever imagined.

▮ *Walk more slowly. Whenever you catch yourself rushing around, slow down. Relax your jaw, drop your shoulder. Breathe. If you have to move quickly, try to do it in this more relaxed way.*

▮ *Talk more slowly. Think about what you are going to say before you say it. Allow yourself to pause and take a breath between sentences or thoughts.*

▮ *When the phone rings, take a deep breath before answering.*

▮ *Take a short break at the same time every day to meditate, breathe or just notice how your body is feeling.*

▮ *Throughout the day, close your eyes for a few moments and visualize yourself in a beautiful place.*

▮ *Use transitions, like travel time to and from your office, to notice how your body is feeling. Try to let go of excess tension before it accumulates.*

▮ *Notice your mindset and body posture when you are driving. Can you be more relaxed when you drive?*

▮ *Go outside at least once a day and pay attention to the weather. Look at the sky, feel the temperature and notice the sensation of the air on your skin.*

▮ *Add something beautiful to your life every day. Put a vase of flowers, a candle or a special drawing in your office, kitchen or space where you spend the most time. Take a picture of one of your favorite places, a gorgeous garden or an ocean landscape, and hang or place it where you can look at it.*

▮ *Spend at least a little time alone every day.*

Reality Check

▮

Use Your Transition Time

If you think you can't find twenty minutes in your day to relax, you are probably the person who needs them most. Try to take a short relaxation break prior to leaving your office, while you're on a train or bus or just after you get home from work. Perhaps there's another natural transition time in your day you haven't thought of before—after the kids leave for school or just before they get home. Look closely at your day and you'll find transition times you never knew you had.

A FEAST FOR THE SENSES

The day is winding down, and it's been one to remember. You've exercised all morning, pampered yourself with sensuous body treatments and spent invaluable time learning how to unwind. You've also eaten the way you've been meaning to for years—a nutritious, substantial breakfast; a light, restorative lunch; and a nourishing snack that boosted your energy. Now you've showered and changed into fresh clothes. You are ready to spend time over dinner connecting with new friends who understand exactly how great you're feeling. At some spas, dinner is very casual. At others, you dress up, order off menus and are served on fine china. At all spas, dinner is treated as the most important meal, an occasion to spend time with friends and talk over the day that's past and the one to come. Dinner caps your day, and it should reflect all that was good about it.

Dinner is the time when spa chefs shine. Their full effort goes into showing how healthful, low-fat food can be innovative, beautiful and pleasing to the palate all at the same time. It's often a gourmet feast, with four full courses—an appetizer, salad, entrée and dessert—that overcome any lingering doubts you might have that healthy can be synonymous with delicious.

Instead of relying on heavy sauces, cream, salt, butter and oil, chefs carefully prepare each dish in a low-fat style, liberally using herbs and spices and imaginatively blending flavors. Sea bass might come with a light sauce of tomato, fennel and saffron, while a seared salmon might be topped with a saffron-citrus sauce spiced with cumin, turmeric and lime. Even a simple penne with chicken relies on garlic, shallots and fresh basil to enhance a tasty blend of red and yellow tomatoes.

At home, you don't have to be a gourmet chef to prepare meals that are equally satisfying. Even if your cooking abilities are undeveloped, there's no reason you and your family should have to eat tasteless food. There are many simple ways to make low-fat meals appealing and pleasurable. For example, besides using herbs and spices, spa chefs are fanatical about the freshness of their ingredients. They use locally grown or produced food whenever possible because the freshest food is also the most flavorful, colorful and nutritious. Following their lead at home may mean stopping by the store more often or searching out a local greenmarket. Even if it takes a little more effort, doing something as simple as using fresh food can make a huge difference in the taste of your meals.

Spa chefs also experiment with exotic grains and unusual fruits and vegetables to give their dishes unpredictable tastes and textures. Pineapple, red onion and peas may be mixed with brown rice for a zesty side dish. An easy-to-cook grain such as kasha can be tossed with soy sauce and vegetables to make an unusual salad. Use a few basic ingredients in creative new ways and you'll soon be nourishing your senses and body at the same time.

Atmosphere can also add to the pleasure of dinner. At the Claremont in Oakland, California, for example, a panoramic view of the ocean and the Golden Gate Bridge at sunset enhances every dinner. The candlelight dinners at Miraval Life in Balance in Tucson and the string quartet at the Doral Golf Resort and Spa in Miami turn healthful meals into romantic repasts. At Rancho La Puerta in Baja, California, crackling fires warm up the dining room on chilly nights and add to the convivial mood. Even the simple kimonos guests wear to dinner at the Golden Door help

turn the evening meal into a festive occasion.

At home, it's all too easy to let breakfast and lunch slip by in a whirlwind schedule. Dinner is your last chance to make dining an occasion. Take it. Turn off the television, put down the magazines and notice your surroundings. Light a candle, turn on some music and put a vase of flowers on the table. Rediscover the art of conversation. Let your family know why you chose this particular dish for dinner, and let them become more involved in future meal planning and preparation. At the very least, you may get them to pay more attention to what they are eating every day.

Even if you are alone for dinner, you can make the occasion special. Put effort into the preparation and presentation of your meals, spending time beforehand thinking about the colors and textures you like. Even if it's only one course, spread out a tablecloth and use a pretty plate. Then spend a few minutes before lifting up your fork paying attention to and appreciating the way your food looks and smells. As you begin to eat, notice the different tastes. Be sure to finish one bite completely before you begin another. Mindful eating like this will add to the enjoyment of your meals.

As you become more discerning about the foods you cook and eat, you also need to become more conscious of portions. Just because a particular food is "healthful" doesn't mean you have carte blanche to eat as much of it as you want. With very few exceptions, you can't eat unlimited quantities of any food and not gain weight. Pasta and bread in particular may be low in fat, but that doesn't mean you can eat two pounds of them in one sitting. Learn to think of food as one of life's supreme pleasures, but, as with most pleasure, best when enjoyed in moderation.

Keep moderation in mind particularly when dining in restaurants where the more-is-better philosophy reigns. In fact, many spas serve dinner restaurant-style not only to give guests a chance to socialize but to introduce them to the satisfying feel of smaller portions. Even at resort spas such as the Crescent Court in Dallas, the Peaks at Telluride in Colorado and the Spa at the Houstonian in Houston, where spa guests order off the same menu as other guests, there are "spa" options, in which the portions and content are carefully controlled.

When dining in restaurants where such options aren't available, you must use your own judgment to make more healthful choices. At spas you can pick up many tips for ordering and dining in restaurants without going overboard.

Even dessert is fine, as long as you eat it in limited quantity. In fact, every spa serves dessert after dinner to make meals complete and satisfying. At some, you'll find small pieces of elaborate concoctions, from chocolate fudge cake to crème brûleé. At others, *dessert* isn't synonymous with fat and sugar, and you'll find lower-calorie selections, such as sorbet, fat-free cheesecake and tiramisu, and fruit-based dishes, such as poached pears in mango sauce. In either case, dessert at spas is savored as an important part of the meal.

After dessert at spas, guests linger for conversation or head off to evening activities—inspirational lectures, workshops or movies. Before bed, there's time for a last dip in the hot tub, a short stroll around the grounds or even a final relaxing massage. The exercise, healthful eating, attention to your body and contemplative time you've worked into the day should have you more relaxed than you've been in a long time. A deep sleep restores you for tomorrow. Make it another spa day.

The Fundamentals of Dinner

Ideally, you strive to eat healthily throughout your day, and dinner is simply an extension of the nutritionally balanced diet you know works best for you. If things don't go exactly the way you planned, however, then look at dinner as the last opportunity to make a difference in the day's diet. If you haven't eaten any fruit or vegetables all day, for example, make up for it in the evening. If lunch consisted of lots of meat or chicken, eat less protein for dinner and focus on grains, pasta or potatoes. Dinner won't subtract calories from a day filled with junk food, but at least it can provide nutrients you still need and haven't gotten. That alone is a good start.

The food pyramid can help. The valuable government guidelines summarized in the pyramid can help you make choices both about foods to include in your diet and how much of them you need. The basic idea behind the pyramid—eat little fat, moderate protein and lots of carbohydrates—seems simple enough. Yet according to spa nutritionists, while parts of the message in the guidelines are being heard, others are either misunderstood or being ignored.

Most people know, for example, about the dangers of including too much fat in their diets. Listed at the tip of the pyramid, fats should be eaten sparingly, whether they are consumed in sauces or dressings or as natural components of foods such as cheese, eggs and meat. People have also learned to cut back on red meat and are eating more fish and poultry. And they have learned that grains, which comprise the base of the pyramid, should make up a large portion of their diets.

What many people have *not* learned is proper food portions and how they relate to overall calories, particularly when it comes to grains. You may understand that a plate of

Deciphering Food Labels

As you begin to follow the guidelines set forth in the pyramid, it will help to know the exact nutritional content of the foods you are buying. These days all cans, cartons, packages and boxes of food have a "nutrition facts" label somewhere on the outside of the packaging. Once you learn how to decipher what it says, you'll know what comprises a serving of that particular food, the number of calories it has, the amount of fat, protein and carbohydrates in it and, most important, what percentages of a variety of daily nutritional requirements this food supplies. Bear in mind that these last percentages are calculated relative to a 2,000 calorie-per-day diet. If yours is less or more, you need to add or subtract accordingly.

Food labels are also important because they address aspects of your diet that are not directly included in the pyramid, such as salt and cholesterol. They also indicate how much of the total fat in the product is saturated, the most important kind to avoid. Even if you don't want or need to calculate every mouthful down to the last percentage point or gram, simply glancing at a label equips you with enough knowledge to make better nutritional choices immediately. Here are some quick tips for interpreting labels offered by the Doral Golf Resort and Spa.

Note what constitutes a serving size. You may end up eating more or less than a serving, but remember that the number of calories, grams of fat and all the other information on that label is calculated according to the amounts in one serving.

To do a quick fat check, see if there are 3 or fewer grams of fat for every 100 calories. For example, if one serving has 200 calories and 6 or fewer grams of fat, it's a low-fat food.

If you're concerned about getting more fiber in your diet, look for foods that have at least 4 to 5 grams per serving. Most have at least some, but those with 4 grams or more per serving are considered "high-fiber foods."

Salt (sodium) amounts are measured in milligrams, so don't be alarmed when you see a number like 200 or 300. There have to be at least 120 milligrams of sodium in a serving before you will even taste it. Up to 2,400 milligrams a day is an acceptable amount for most healthy people.

Look closely at the sugar content. You may be eating more sugar than you think, since it is often hidden in foods you don't even consider sweet. To give yourself a reality check, divide the number of grams listed per serving by four. That is the number of teaspoons of sugar in one serving.

pasta with tomato-based primavera sauce is lower in calories than one with cream sauce. But you still need to consider the amount you are eating. A big plate of pasta is still BIG—and that translates into plenty of calories. Remember, your weight is determined by the total number of calories you consume in a day, not by just the amount of fat.

The pyramid guidelines recommend that you have six to eleven servings of grains, cereal and pasta each day, but remember, one serving is just half a cup of cooked pasta or rice. A big bowl of pasta served in a restaurant may have all the grain requirements you need for an entire day. The same is true for dishes that contain rice, bread or cereal. Maybe you like to eat two or three pieces of bread before a risotto dinner and think it's okay because you don't add butter. Consider that three pieces of bread along with a large bowl of risotto may add up to more servings of grains than you need in a day, as well as plenty of calories. If you had a big bowl of cereal for breakfast and a sandwich for lunch, you might be better off substituting a piece of chicken or fish.

Even as people continue to load up on starches such as pasta and bread, they are still not making enough choices from the food groups in the middle of the pyramid—fruits and vegetables. According to the government guidelines, you need two to four servings of fruit and three to five servings of vegetables every day. If you, like many other people, just don't get enough, dinner is the perfect time to get them into your diet by combining them with other foods. Meat or grains go beautifully with vegetables and can be equally enhanced with fruit relishes or sauces.

Whether you dine out or cook at home,

healthful eating is about striving for balance. Spa nutritionists suggest that instead of making drastic dietary changes all at once, you make them slowly. Start by looking at what you eat over the course of a day or week, then think about foods to cut back on and others to add. Think as well about how *much* you're eating. That alone can make a big difference. And remember, even if you use the pyramid as a guide, there's lots of room for personal choice and invention.

> **"Fat-free is not the end-all. Whatever happened to real nutrition?"**
> Deborah Daley, nutritionist, Doral Golf Resort and Spa

Putting the Pleasure Back in Food

No matter who you are, what you do or where you live, eating is not just a necessity of life but one of its greatest sources of pleasure. It isn't a bad habit that you should quit, but from the way many people deprive themselves, that is what it seems like they are trying to do.

How many times have you heard someone label a food "good" or "bad"? Maybe you've done it yourself. Ice cream has fat and sugar, therefore it must be "bad." On the other hand, squash has few calories and lots of nutrients, so it must be "good." When you label food this way, you set yourself up for punishment every time you eat something you view as bad. Some people actually label a day as a success or failure according to whether they've eaten the "right" foods or the "wrong" ones.

Try looking at food from a new perspective. You are going to have to eat for as long as you live. That means that the bond you form with food is one of the most important you'll ever make. There's little satisfaction if that bond is based on denial and guilt, because you're always depriving yourself of certain foods and letting guilt replace pleasure when you do eat them. It's equally unsatisfying to view eating particular foods as chores, something you have to do but can't enjoy. One way or the other, you take all the pleasure out of eating.

Nutrition specialists at spas such as Green Mountain at Fox Run in Ludlow, Vermont, the PGA National Resort and Spa in Palm Beach Gardens, Florida, and the Doral Golf Resort and Spa in Miami teach guests that food misconceptions like these are very common and that it's time to start thinking in other ways. By discovering foods and preparing meals that are nourishing to your senses and body at the same time, you'll find your attitude toward food slowly changing. The following are these spas' suggestions to help you form a more positive bond with food and put the pleasure back into dining.

Do a little tinkering with your mindset. Quit thinking of foods as "good" or "bad." For instance, cake, ice cream and French fries may be three of your favorite foods. But if you also see them as "bad" and cut them out of your diet completely, you link guilt to pleasure. You punish yourself mentally when you break down and indulge and automatically ruin any enjoyment these foods might have brought you. Instead, try thinking of them as "occasional" treats, foods you won't eat every day but, when you do, you'll love every bite.

Eat foods you really like. This is essential if you want to develop a healthy relationship with food. Just because you've heard that broccoli is good for you doesn't mean you have to eat it if you dislike it. There are plenty of other green vegetables, and some are bound to be more pleasing to your palate. There is huge variety within every food group, and it should be possible for you to find grains, fruits, vegetables, lean meats and dairy products that you like. Out of these, you can build a base of "everyday" foods you really enjoy.

Find the freshest food possible. In-season produce is best. Buying fruit just off the tree or vegetables and herbs right out of the ground improves the color and taste of your meals, which in turn adds pleasure to your eating. Don't overlook frozen food, though. Freezing is usually done immediately after picking, thus locking in nutrients and taste. Shop the periphery of supermarkets. That's where you'll find the freshest and least-processed foods. Try to weed out any foods that have been highly processed. A good rule to follow: If the label has a long list of unrecognizable ingredients with complicated names, put it back.

Fill your refrigerator with color. Nutritionists repeatedly emphasize the importance of a colorful diet. Open your refrigerator and see how many colorful foods it holds. Visualize what you normally eat and see if there's a wide range of colors represented. Foods that are rich in color tend to be rich in nutrients. They will also please both your eye and your tastebuds.

Discover natural flavors. Avoid heavy sauces and rich cream dressings that disguise the natural taste of fresh produce. If you've never had asparagus without hollandaise sauce, you probably don't know how it really tastes. Cut back on salt and pepper, too, and discover how delicious your favorite vegetables can be all by themselves.

Challenge your tastebuds. Experiment with seasonings other than salt and pepper. Oregano, basil, thyme, rosemary, cayenne and sage can really add life to your meals, particularly in their freshest state. Look for recipes that incorporate spices or herbs you haven't tried. It can be a sensory experience just to cook with new ingredients like these.

The Variety of Tastes

Sharpening your sense of taste can help you find greater pleasure in your meals. In general, foods come in six different tastes: pungent, sweet, sour, salty, bitter and astringent. A seventh, known as umami, is the Japanese word for oily. To be fully satisfying, each dinner you eat ideally should incorporate as many of these tastes as possible. That isn't as difficult as it sounds, since many foods already have two or more tastes. Balancing tastes in a meal may be something you are already doing instinctively. The following information, given to guests at Lake Austin Spa Resort in Austin, Texas, will help you learn more about which foods are usually associated with which tastes:

FRUITS: mainly sweet and astringent; citrus adds a sour taste.

VEGETABLES: mainly sweet and astringent; leafy greens are also bitter.

DAIRY: mainly sweet; yogurt and cheese are also sour and astringent.

OILS: sweet, but the Japanese would say "umami."

GRAINS AND NUTS: mainly sweet.

LEGUMES: sweet and astringent.

HERBS AND SPICES: mainly pungent; some are sweet; others have an astringent and bitter taste.

MEATS: sweet and astringent.

These are some foods that fall into specific taste categories:

SWEET: sugar, honey, rice, milk, cream, butter, carrots, beets

SALTY: salt

SOUR: lemons, cheese, yogurt, tomatoes, grapes, plums, sour fruit, vinegar

BITTER: bitter greens (endive, chicory, romaine lettuce), tonic water, lemon rind, spinach, leafy greens, turmeric, fenugreek, parsley, coffee, sesame seeds, saccharin.

PUNGENT: cayenne, chili peppers, onions, garlic, radishes, ginger, thyme, oregano, sunflower sprouts, spicy food in general, cumin, anise, saffron

Entrées— Meat, Poultry and Fish

What's for dinner? More often than not, spas serve poultry and fish when they're not opting for vegetarian entrées. Some spas these days also serve lean cuts of beef, pork and lamb. The difference between these meals and the classic American meat-and-potatoes dinner is that at spas the emphasis will be on the "potatoes," not the "meat." Your plate will contain a small portion of meat, accompanied by flavorful grains and a variety of vegetables. Whenever possible, vegetables play a central role in recipes, even meat-oriented dishes such as braised beef tenderloin and loin of lamb.

From marinades before cooking to piquant sauces added after, spa chefs have found ingenious ways to make poultry, fish and meat flavorful without adding fat. They choose the leanest cuts and remove visible fat from meat and skin from chicken prior to cooking. Then, instead of sautéing or frying in butter or oil, they poach, broil, grill, roast, bake and stew, letting meat and poultry simmer in their own juices for extra moisture and tenderness. Sometimes they cook the meat along with vegetables for even more flavor. All-time favorites such as fried chicken are deliciously imitated by rolling the pieces in a special batter and then baking.

Spices and herbs are important for making rich-tasting sauces without butter or cream, but fresh or dried fruit can be just as enticing. In fact, lemon and orange slices are commonly used as toppings for fish or chicken. It's amazing how something as simple as freshly squeezed lemon juice can give a dish plenty of zest. See for yourself how different your dinners can be by experimenting with these favorite spa recipes.

GRILLED LOIN OF SONOMA LAMB
with Moroccan Barbecue Sauce and Dried Fruit Couscous
from the ISPA Collaboration

4 five-ounce lamb loin medallions or
well-trimmed loin chops
Salt and ground black pepper to taste
1 pound snow peas or sugar snap peas
1 cup Moroccan Barbecue Sauce (*see below*)
Dried Fruit Couscous (*see page 135*)
Assorted fresh herbs for garnish

1. Preheat grill or broiler. Season lamb with salt and pepper.
2. Grill or broil for about 4 minutes per side for medium-rare meat, or until desired doneness. If desired, cut each medallion into 4 slices.
3. Cook snow peas in boiling water for 2 to 3 minutes. Drain.
4. To serve, place ¼ cup Barbecue Sauce on each plate and top with lamb. Arrange Dried Fruit Couscous and snow peas around lamb. Garnish with fresh herbs.
Makes 4 servings

MOROCCAN BARBECUE SAUCE
2 large tomatoes, chopped
1 star anise
1 teaspoon chili paste or chili powder
1 cinnamon stick
¼ cup orange juice
¼ cup honey
1 teaspoon grated ginger
2 teaspoons minced garlic
1 teaspoon sesame oil

2 teaspoons red wine vinegar

$1/2$ large onion, chopped

$1/2$ teaspoon cumin seed

1. Place all ingredients in a large saucepan over low heat. Simmer for 1 hour.

2. Remove star anise and cinnamon stick.

3. Process in a food processor or blender in batches until smooth.

Makes about 1 cup

DRIED FRUIT COUSCOUS

$1/2$ cup instant couscous

$1/4$ cup chopped, dried fruit, such as raisins, apricots, dates, or figs

1 teaspoon chopped fresh mint

1 teaspoon sesame oil

Salt and ground black pepper to taste

1. Prepare couscous according to package directions.

2. Stir in remaining ingredients until well combined.

Makes 4 servings

BRAISED BEEF TENDERLOIN "À LA FICELLE"

from the ISPA Collaboration

2 quarts low-salt, low-fat chicken stock or broth

1 large head cabbage, cut into 8 pieces

4 medium carrots, peeled and cut into chunks

4 ribs celery, cut into 1-inch pieces

2 large zucchini, cut into 1-inch pieces

1 large turnip, peeled and cut into 1-inch pieces

1 large leek, cut into pieces

2 pounds center-cut beef tenderloin

Chopped parsley for garnish

1. In a large saucepot or Dutch oven, simmer stock over medium heat.

2. One at a time, poach vegetables in hot stock until crisp-tender. Remove and set aside.

3. In same stock, place beef tenderloin. Cover and simmer 20 minutes for rare meat, or until desired doneness. Remove meat, reserving stock.

4. Cut meat crosswise into 8 portions.

5. If necessary, briefly return vegetables to stock to reheat.

6. To serve, place cabbage wedges in soup plates and top with beef and remaining vegetables. Pour in stock to almost cover. Sprinkle with parsley.

Makes 8 servings

GRILLED TURKEY PAILLARD
with Orange Chili Glaze and White Grape Relish

from the Doral Golf Resort and Spa

An 8-ounce boneless, skinless turkey breast, cut into 4 portions

Orange Chili Glaze (*see page 136*)

White Grape Relish (*see page 136*)

1. Preheat grill.

2. Flatten turkey breast pieces to $1/4$-inch thickness.

3. Grill turkey for approximately 5 minutes per side. Turn midway through. Brush with hot Orange Chili Glaze while cooking.

4. Serve with White Grape Relish and additional Orange Chili Glaze.

Makes 4 servings

NOTE: Serve this with Maple Mashed Sweet Potatoes (*see recipe page 141*).

ORANGE CHILI GLAZE

1 tablespoon corn oil

1 medium onion, diced

1 tablespoon minced garlic

3 serrano chili peppers, diced

1 tablespoon coriander seed

2 tablespoons chili powder

1 tablespoon ground cumin

$1/2$ cup fresh orange juice

2 tablespoons molasses

$1/2$ cup rice wine vinegar

$1/2$ cup chicken stock

2 tablespoons arrowroot, mixed with $1/4$ cup water

2 tablespoons chopped cilantro

1. Heat oil in a saucepan. Cook onion and garlic until tender.

2. Add remaining ingredients except arrowroot and cilantro and bring to a boil.

3. Add arrowroot/water mixture and mix well. Simmer for about 5 minutes.

4. Stir in cilantro.

Makes about 1$1/2$ cups

WHITE GRAPE RELISH

$1/4$ cup dried cranberries

$1/4$ cup white wine

1$1/2$ tablespoons honey

$1/4$ cup orange juice

8 ounces white (green) grapes

1 tablespoon lime juice

Combine ingredients in a saucepan and cook on low heat until mixture forms a chutney-like consistency and fruit is tender, about 45 minutes.

Makes $3/4$ cup

SOUTHWESTERN OVEN-FRIED CHICKEN

with Roasted Red Pepper Puree

from the ISPA Collaboration

$1/3$ cup whole-wheat flour

2 egg whites, lightly beaten

1 cup cornflake crumbs

1 teaspoon garlic powder

1 teaspoon chili powder

1 teaspoon ground cumin

Roasted Red Pepper Puree (*see below*)

3 boneless, skinless chicken breasts, halved

1. Preheat oven to 375°F. Spray a baking sheet with nonstick cooking spray.

2. Spread flour on waxed paper. Put egg whites in a shallow dish. Mix cornflake crumbs, garlic powder, chili powder, and cumin. Place on another piece of waxed paper.

3. Coat each piece of chicken in flour. Dip in egg whites, then in cornflake crumb mixture, patting to coat well.

4. Place on prepared baking sheet.

5. Bake for 20 to 30 minutes, or until tender.

6. Serve with Roasted Red Pepper Puree.

Makes 6 servings

ROASTED RED PEPPER PUREE

1 large onion, chopped

4 cloves garlic, minced

5 red peppers, roasted, seeded, peeled, and cut into 1-inch pieces

4 cups low-salt, low-fat chicken stock or bouillon

1 teaspoon ground cumin

1 smoked chipotle pepper

1 teaspoon sea salt

1. Spray a nonstick saucepan with nonstick cooking spray. Over medium-high heat, cook onion and garlic until tender.

2. Add red pepper and cook for 1 minute.

3. Add stock and remaining ingredients. Bring to a boil. Reduce heat to low and simmer for 10 minutes. Cool slightly.

4. Blend mixture in a food processor or blender until smooth. Return to saucepan. Cook until mixture reaches desired thickness.

SEARED SALMON
with Saffron-Citrus Sauce
from the ISPA Collaboration

2 tablespoons olive oil

2 tablespoons chopped garlic

1 tablespoon ground cumin

2 teaspoons ground turmeric

10 to 15 saffron strands

3/4 cup orange juice

1/2 cup lime juice

5 tablespoons white zinfandel

2 medium yellow peppers, seeded and chopped

1 small yellow tomato, chopped

4 cups vegetable stock or broth

2 tablespoons cornstarch

Salt to taste

8 three-ounce boneless, skinless salmon fillets

1. Preheat oven to 375°F.

2. Put oil in a deep-sided sauté pan over medium-high heat. Add garlic, cumin, turmeric, and saffron. Cook for 2 minutes. Add orange juice, lime juice, zinfandel, peppers, and tomato. Cook until reduced by three-quarters. Add vegetable stock. Cook until reduced by one-quarter.

3. In a small bowl, mix cornstarch with 2 tablespoons water. Add to sauce. Cook, stirring, until thickened.

4. Strain sauce through fine sieve or cheesecloth. Season with salt. Keep warm.

5. Spray oven-proof nonstick skillet with nonstick cooking spray. Place over high heat.

6. Add salmon fillets. Cook until seared, turning once.

7. Put skillet in oven and bake for 6 minutes, or until desired doneness.

8. To serve, place salmon on plates. Top with sauce.

Makes 8 servings

LEMON CHICKEN
from the Cooper Aerobics Center

1 tablespoon grated lemon rind

1/2 cup lemon juice

2 tablespoons water

2 tablespoons corn oil

2 teaspoons soy sauce

1 clove garlic, minced

1/2 teaspoon salt

1/2 teaspoon ground black pepper

6 four-ounce boneless, skinless chicken breasts

1/2 cup flour

1 teaspoon paprika

1. Mix lemon rind and juice, water, oil, soy sauce, garlic, salt, and pepper. Pour over chicken. Cover and refrigerate for at least 3 hours or overnight.

2. Preheat oven to 400°F.

3. Drain chicken, reserving marinade. Combine flour with paprika in a shallow dish and coat chicken. Shake off excess.

4. Spray a shallow baking pan with nonstick cooking spray. Place chicken in a single layer in pan and bake for 15 minutes.

5. Turn chicken. Pour marinade over chicken. Bake for 10 to 15 minutes more, or until tender, basting occasionally with marinade in pan.

Makes 6 servings

Grains and Pastas

Easy to make, inexpensive and low in fat, pasta, rice and other grains complement meat, poultry and fish or stand on their own as substantial dinner dishes. Spa chefs use grains and pastas in highly creative ways, mixing in vegetables, fresh herbs and even fruit for colorful, enticing meals. By adding a little meat or cheese to grains, you can make a balanced one-dish dinner that is simple to prepare. Fresh white, whole-wheat and vegetable pastas are available at supermarkets these days, as are scores of dried varieties. It's also much easier now to find grains such as couscous, quinoa and kasha, as well as wild, jasmine or basmati rice, all flavorful options that can add new tastes and textures to your cooking without extra time or effort. Whenever possible, choose whole-grain or brown varieties for added fiber and nutrition. Following are some favorite spa recipes for grain and pasta dishes.

TUSCANY-STYLE PASTA
with Eggplant, Zucchini, Tomato, and Fresh Herbs
from the ISPA Collaboration

1 tablespoon olive oil

1 medium eggplant, peeled and cut into $^1/_2$-inch cubes

2 cloves garlic, minced

$^1/_2$ cup red wine

A 28-ounce can whole tomatoes, with juice

4 large button mushrooms, cut into quarters

2 ribs celery, sliced into $^1/_2$-inch pieces

1 large red pepper, seeded and cut into $^1/_2$-inch pieces

1 yellow squash, cut into $^1/_2$-inch cubes

1 tablespoon chopped fresh oregano or 1 teaspoon dried

1 tablespoon chopped fresh basil or 1 teaspoon dried

$^1/_4$ teaspoon salt

$^1/_4$ teaspoon freshly ground black pepper

1 pound linguini or spinach fettuccine

2 tablespoons grated Parmesan cheese

1. Heat oil in a large skillet over medium heat. Add eggplant and garlic. Cover and cook for 7 minutes.

2. Reduce heat to low. Add red wine. Cook for 2 minutes. Add remaining ingredients except pasta and Parmesan cheese. Cover and simmer for 20 minutes, or until vegetables are tender.

3. Prepare linguini according to package directions. Drain.

4. Top linguini with sauce and sprinkle Parmesan cheese on top.

Makes 6 servings

ITALIAN PESTO
from the PGA National Resort and Spa

2 cups fresh basil leaves

4 cloves garlic, coarsely chopped

1/4 cup fresh Italian parsley

1/4 cup fresh mint leaves (optional)

1/4 cup grated Parmesan cheese

1/4 cup water

2 tablespoons pine nuts

2 tablespoons grated Romano cheese

1 tablespoon olive oil

1. Place all ingredients in a blender or food processor and puree until smooth. For thinner pesto, add water until desired consistency is reached.

2. Store in refrigerator for up to 1 week.

Makes 1 cup

MARINARA SAUCE
from the Golden Door

1 tablespoon olive oil

1 small white onion, diced

4 cloves garlic, minced

2 pounds plum tomatoes, peeled, seeded, and diced, or two 28-ounce cans plum tomatoes, drained and diced

1 cup tomato puree (canned or fresh)

2 teaspoons minced fresh thyme

1 tablespoon minced fresh oregano

1 whole bay leaf

1 teaspoon sugar (optional)

1 cup fresh basil leaves, measured and then cut into strips

Ground black pepper to taste

1. Heat oil over medium heat in a deep-sided sauté pan.

2. Add onion and garlic. Stir until soft.

3. Add plum tomatoes, tomato puree, thyme, oregano, bay leaf, and sugar. Cook for approximately 45 minutes over medium heat, stirring occasionally. Sauce should be thick.

4. Remove bay leaf. Add basil and black pepper.

Makes 3 cups

SPINACH, MUSHROOM, AND ZUCCHINI LASAGNA
from the Golden Door

1 pound lasagna noodles

2 fifteen-ounce containers low-fat ricotta cheese

5 bunches fresh spinach, cooked (2 1/2 cups after cooking)

1 teaspoon ground black pepper, plus additional for sprinkling

1/8 teaspoon ground nutmeg

3 cups sliced zucchini

5 cups sliced button mushrooms

1 tablespoon minced garlic

1 to 2 tablespoons vegetable broth or water

2 1/2 cups Marinara Sauce (*see above*)

1/4 cup fresh basil or oregano, minced

4 ounces asiago, mozzarella, or Parmesan cheese, grated

1. Bring a large pot of water to a boil and cook lasagna noodles for about 10 minutes. Drain, rinse and set aside.

2. Combine ricotta cheese and spinach in a food processor and process briefly. Season with pepper and nutmeg. Set aside.

3. Heat a nonstick pan over medium heat, spray with nonstick spray, and sauté zucchini until it begins to soften. Remove zucchini and set aside.

4. Wipe pan clean, heat again, and spray with nonstick spray. Sauté mushrooms and garlic with a sprinkle of black pepper until mushrooms are soft. When mushrooms begin to stick to pan, add vegetable broth or water. Remove from heat.

5. Stir fresh basil or oregano into Marinara Sauce.

6. Preheat oven to 350°F.

7. To assemble: Spread about ½ cup Marinara Sauce in bottom of 10-by-14-inch glass pan. Layer one-third of cooked noodles across bottom, then layer in the following order: one-half ricotta/spinach mixture, one-half cooked mushrooms, one-half cooked zucchini, and one-half Marinara Sauce. Repeat, beginning and ending with a layer of noodles. Cover with remaining Marinara Sauce. Sprinkle grated cheese on top.

8. Bake for 20 to 30 minutes.
Makes 15 servings

CARIBBEAN FRIED RICE
from the PGA National Resort and Spa

1 teaspoon sesame oil

¼ cup diced red pepper

¼ cup sliced button mushrooms

2 tablespoons frozen peas

3 tablespoons diced pineapple, fresh or canned

2 tablespoons diced red onion

1 tablespoon chopped cilantro

3½ cups unsalted cooked brown rice

¼ cup low-sodium chicken broth

¼ cup lite soy sauce

1. In a large skillet over medium heat, heat sesame oil. Sauté pepper, mushrooms, peas, pineapple, onion, and cilantro until onion is translucent, stirring occasionally.

2. Add remaining ingredients. Cook until liquid is absorbed, stirring occasionally.
Makes 4½ cups

KASHA SALAD
from the ISPA Collaboration

2 cups vegetable stock or water

1 cup uncooked kasha

2 tablespoons lite soy sauce

1 teaspoon ground cumin

3 cloves garlic, minced

1 medium carrot, peeled and finely chopped

1 rib celery, finely chopped

1 small onion, finely chopped

1 pimiento, chopped

½ cup lime juice

2 tablespoons teriyaki sauce

1 tablespoon chopped fresh dill

Ground black pepper to taste

1. Place vegetable stock, kasha, soy sauce, and cumin in a medium skillet. Bring to a boil. Reduce heat to low. Cover and simmer for 30 minutes, or until kasha is tender and liquid is absorbed.

2. Place remaining ingredients in a large bowl. Add cooked kasha and toss until well combined.

3. Cover and refrigerate for at least 30 minutes.
Makes 6 servings

Creative Potatoes

With potatoes you can be as innovative as you like, adding any number of flavors, textures or colors. Spa chefs dress them up with almost anything but lots of butter, sour cream or other high-fat condiments. By scooping out the inside of a baked potato, mixing it with chopped vegetables, onions, herbs and a sprinkling of cheese, you have a nicely balanced dish that can serve as a light dinner on its own. Try topping your potatoes with creamy yogurt, spicy salsa or even a thick bean soup. If you prefer, mash and mix them spa-style. Try these delicious varieties.

MAPLE MASHED SWEET POTATOES
from the Doral Golf Resort and Spa

2 pounds sweet potatoes
2 tablespoons butter
6 ounces evaporated skim milk
2 tablespoons honey

1. Peel sweet potatoes and cut into large slices.
2. Cover with water in a large stock pot and bring to a boil. Reduce heat and simmer until potatoes are soft. Drain.
3. Mash potatoes in large bowl.
4. Add remaining ingredients and blend well.

Makes 10 servings

AUTHORS' NOTE: For a change, try this healthful dish as a substitute for regular potatoes when serving turkey, chicken, or red meat.

TWICE-BAKED POTATOES
from the PGA National Resort and Spa

2 large Idaho potatoes, washed
$1/2$ cup low-fat cottage cheese
3 tablespoons grated Parmesan cheese
1 small onion, diced
2 cloves garlic, minced

2 teaspoons olive oil
$3/4$ of a 10-ounce package of frozen chopped spinach, thawed and drained
2 green onions, chopped
1 tablespoon chopped fresh parsley or 1 teaspoon dried
1 tablespoon chopped fresh basil or 1 teaspoon dried
$1/2$ teaspoon ground white pepper
$1/4$ teaspoon ground red pepper
1 teaspoon paprika

1. Preheat oven to 400°F.
2. Pierce potatoes and bake for 1 hour, or until fork-tender. Cool.
3. Cut in half lengthwise. Scoop out flesh, leaving 1/2 inch of potato in shells. Set shells aside.
4. Lower oven temperature to 350°F.
5. In medium bowl, mash scooped potato with cheeses.
6. In a large skillet over medium heat, sauté onion and garlic in oil until onion is translucent. Add spinach. Cook for 2 minutes. Remove from heat.
7. Combine spinach-onion mixture, green onions, parsley, basil, peppers, and mashed potato mixture. Beat until well mixed. Spoon or pipe potato mixture into reserved potato shells.
8. Bake for 15 minutes, until tops are lightly browned and crispy.

Makes 4 servings

▮Delectable Guiltless Desserts

You'll find dessert served at virtually every spa you visit. Something sweet at the end of dinner makes a meal more satisfying, and many people feel deprived if they don't get it. At home, there's no reason to forgo this pleasurable course even if you are seriously watching your weight.

Dessert doesn't always have to be high in fat and calories. Low-fat and low-calorie ice cream, cookies and even pastries are creating a booming business everywhere. Many are so good, your family won't be able to tell them apart from regular high-fat, high-calorie varieties. If you prefer homemade desserts, consider something fruit-based. Sorbet, strawberries on angel food cake and even sliced pineapple or frozen grapes will soothe a sweet tooth without adding a lot of fat.

Even high-fat, high-calorie desserts don't have to be taboo if the portions are small. Many spas have desserts as decadent as any you'll find at a French pastry shop. But cookies are small, slices of cake are thin and guests may get only a taste or two of ice cream rather than huge scoops.

If dessert is something you enjoy and want to continue eating throughout your life, there's no reason not to. Keep servings small, and use enticing recipes such as these from spas around the country.

FLAN
from the Lake Austin Spa Resort

¹/₂ cup water

1¹/₂ cups brown sugar

3 eggs

4 egg whites

2 teaspoons vanilla extract

2 cups 1-percent milk

6 ounces evaporated skim milk

2 teaspoons cornstarch, dissolved in a little milk

7 ounces fat-free sweetened condensed milk

2 tablespoons sugar

4 ounces low-fat cream cheese, softened

4 ounces fat-free cream cheese, softened

1. Preheat oven to 325°F. Combine water and sugar in a saucepan. Bring to a boil, reduce heat, and simmer, stirring occasionally, for 5 minutes.

2. Divide sugar among 12 individual oven-proof dessert cups or pour into a 13 x 9-inch rectangular baking pan.

3. Combine remaining ingredients in a food processor and blend until smooth. Pour into dessert cups or baking pan. Set cups or baking pan into a larger pan. Add water to larger pan to a depth of 1 inch. Bake until set, about 1 hour for cups and 1¹/₂ hours for baking pan. As water depth drops below 1 inch during baking, add extra water to larger pan.

4. Carefully remove from water bath and chill. To unmold, run a sharp knife around the edge and invert flan onto plates or platter.
Makes 12 servings

FAT-FREE HOT FUDGE PUDDING CAKE

from the Cooper Aerobics Center

1¼ cups sugar

1 cup flour

7 tablespoons cocoa powder

2 teaspoons baking powder

¼ teaspoon salt

½ cup skim milk

⅓ cup applesauce

1½ teaspoons vanilla extract

½ cup firmly packed brown sugar

1¼ cups hot water

1. Preheat oven to 350°F.

2. In a medium bowl, combine ¾ cup of the sugar with the flour, 3 tablespoons of the cocoa powder, baking powder, and salt. Blend in milk, applesauce, and vanilla. Beat until smooth. Pour into an 8- or 9-inch square pan.

3. In a small bowl, combine remaining ½ cup sugar, the brown sugar, and the remaining 4 tablespoons cocoa powder. Sprinkle mixture evenly over top.

4. Pour hot water over top. Do not stir. Bake for 40 minutes, or until the center is almost set. Let stand for 15 minutes.

5. Spoon into dessert dishes, spooning sauce from bottom of pan over top.

Makes 10 servings

AUTHORS' NOTE: This gooey dessert will satisfy any sweet tooth. To make it less sweet, cut back on sugar.

CHEESECAKE

from the Doral Golf Resort and Spa

3 cups low-fat cottage cheese

1 cup plain low-fat yogurt

8 ounces fat-free cream cheese

2 tablespoons arrowroot

1 cup sugar

1 tablespoon vanilla extract

2 teaspoons orange zest

1 teaspoon lemon zest

Pinch of salt

⅓ cup graham cracker crumbs

¼ cup chocolate syrup (optional)

1. Preheat oven to 325°F.

2. Combine all ingredients except graham cracker crumbs and chocolate syrup in a food processor. Process until smooth.

3. Coat a 10-inch cake pan with nonstick cooking spray and dust with graham cracker crumbs.

4. Pour batter over crumbs.

5. Drizzle chocolate syrup in center of cake and swirl with a toothpick to create a design.

3. Place cake pan in a large shallow baking pan. Add water to larger pan to fill halfway. Bake for 1½ hours, or until middle is set. Add water to baking pan during baking when level gets low.

7. Remove from water bath and chill.

Makes 12 servings

PUMPKIN COOKIES

from Green Valley Spa and Tennis Resort

A 10-ounce can pumpkin

1 cup honey

5 egg whites

An 8-ounce can applesauce

3 cups whole-wheat flour

1 tablespoon baking powder

$^1/_2$ tablespoon baking soda

$^1/_2$ teaspoon ground nutmeg

$^1/_2$ teaspoon ground ginger

$^1/_2$ cup raisins

$^1/_2$ cup chopped walnuts

1. Preheat oven to 400°F.

2. Mix together pumpkin, honey, egg whites, and applesauce. Add flour, baking powder, baking soda, nutmeg, ginger, raisins, and nuts.

3. Drop by teaspoonful onto cookie sheets. Bake for 10 minutes. Cool on a wire rack.

Makes 3 dozen

MICHEL'S OATMEAL COOKIES

from the Golden Door

2 whole eggs

2 egg whites

1 teaspoon cinnamon

1 teaspoon vanilla extract

1 teaspoon salt

1 teaspoon baking powder

1 cup granulated sugar

$^1/_2$ cup brown sugar

$3^1/_4$ cups rolled oats

$^1/_3$ cup whole-wheat flour

1. Preheat oven to 375°F.

2. In a mixing bowl, beat eggs, egg whites, cinnamon, vanilla, salt, baking powder, and sugars at high speed until volume doubles in size.

3. Fold rolled oats and flour into mixture.

4. Spray pan or cookie sheet with nonstick cooking spray. Drop mixture onto pan or sheet by tablespoonsful. Allow adequate space between cookies for spreading.

5. Bake for 15 to 20 minutes. Remove from cookie sheets immediately.

Makes 4 dozen

FUDGE BROWNIES

from Canyon Ranch

2 ounces semisweet chocolate

3 tablespoons salted butter

2 tablespoons vegetable oil

1 cup sugar

1 cup flour

5 tablespoons cocoa powder

$^1/_2$ teaspoon baking powder

Pinch of salt

2 tablespoons apricot preserves

3 egg whites

$^1/_4$ cup Nonfat Fudge Sauce (*see page 145*)

1. Preheat oven to 325°F. Lightly spray an 8 x 8-inch pan with nonstick cooking spray.

2. In a small saucepan over low heat, melt chocolate, butter, and oil. Remove from heat and set aside.

3. In a medium bowl, mix together $^1/_2$ cup of the sugar with the flour, cocoa powder, baking powder, and salt. Add apricot preserves and mix well.

4. In a separate bowl, whip egg whites and remaining $^1/_2$ cup sugar until soft peaks are formed. Gently fold half of chocolate mixture into egg whites. Fold in remaining chocolate mixture. Fold flour mixture into chocolate mixture.

5. Pour batter into prepared pan and bake for 30 minutes, or until knife comes out clean when inserted in middle.

6. Remove from oven. Cool slightly. Drizzle with Nonfat Fudge Sauce.

Makes 12 servings

NONFAT FUDGE SAUCE

1/2 cup powdered sugar

1 tablespoon cocoa powder

1 tablespoon skim milk

Mix all ingredients together in a small bowl.
Makes 1/4 cup

▮Dining Out without Overdoing It

Dinner is the time many choose for socializing, doing business or just taking time out. How many times have you thought you could lose weight easily if you could only quit eating out so often? Yet eating dinner in today's restaurants doesn't have to be an excuse for overeating or loading up on fat and calories. Restaurants are more health-conscious than ever before. Almost all of them, from fast food to gourmet, have low-fat, nutritious options.

Dinner is served restaurant-style at many spas in part to give guests a feel for how to order and how much to order when they dine out. You'll find many suggestions at spas for ways to avoid such pitfalls as ordering too much food, equating dining out with overindulging and not knowing the best low-fat options on the menu. Here are a few of their suggestions:

▮ *Eat a low-calorie snack late in the afternoon. Feeling famished at a restaurant invites trouble. A piece of fruit or some crackers will keep hunger pangs at bay.*

▮ *If you are very hungry when you first arrive at a restaurant, order some soup, a salad or some raw vegetables immediately. Having something nutritious to eat right away will help you stay away from bread, chips and nuts. Salty appetizers prompt you to eat more.*

▮ *Avoid alcohol on an empty stomach. If you want wine or beer, have it with dinner. Drinking alcohol when you are hungry can increase your appetite.*

▮ *Order foods that take a long time to eat. Steamed clams, shelled crab, cioppino and artichokes are all foods that make you work for every bite.*

▮ *If you are served more food than you want to eat, have the waiter wrap half to take home, give it to a hungry companion or offer "tastes" all around.*

▮ *Order a soup or salad as an appetizer and an appetizer as an entrée. If you order a regular entrée, eat a green salad or bowl of soup first.*

▮ *Don't be afraid to make special requests. Ask to have the skin removed from chicken or fish. Get sauces and dressings on the side. Have meat broiled instead of fried. Ask for baked potatoes, rice or even fruit in place of French fries or creamy side dishes. Restaurants are used to accommodating their customers and will rarely turn down a simple request.*

■ *Exchange cottage cheese for butter on potatoes, and use low-fat condiments such as mustard in place of mayonnaise or sour cream.*

■ *Ask if you can order a half-portion of high-fat dishes, or split them with your companions.*

■ *Practice leaving a small portion of food on your plate.*

■ *When you have had enough, ask to have your plate removed immediately to keep yourself from nibbling.*

■ *Be careful not to order too much food. Start small, and order something else if you are still hungry.*

■ *At a buffet or cafeteria, use a salad plate instead of a dinner plate. This helps keep portions small.*

■ *Slow down. Chew slowly, and finish every bite before you take another. Slowing down helps your digestion and gives you a chance to know when you've had enough.*

■ Eating Mindfully

A philosophy of "mindfulness," or paying attention to your moment-to-moment experience, is showing up at many spas these days, most often as a method of stress reduction. At Miraval Life in Balance, mindful eating is taught as a way to help guests become aware of the sensations and feelings they associate with eating, which can lead to richer experiences with food and greater enjoyment of meals. Here are a number of suggestions for practicing mindful eating during dinner.

■ **Awaken your senses.** *Start by spending a few moments in silence at the beginning of a meal. If you are with another person, agree that you won't begin talking for five minutes. Use the first moments of your quiet time to be thankful for the food you are about to eat.*

Next, take another minute or so to simply look at the food in front of you. Do you like the color, form and texture? Eating involves all your senses, and mindful eating can put you in touch with each one. After you start to eat, notice the smell, taste, texture and even sound of your food. Maybe you've always loved chutney, but have you ever thought specifically about why you love it? Is it the consistency, the blend of colors or the combination of sweet and sour tastes? Concentrating on the effects foods have on your senses will give you a deeper understanding of why you like and dislike certain foods. You can use that information to make better choices.

When you finally do begin speaking, spend a few minutes talking only about the food. As you turn your attention to other topics, try to continue noticing the food as well. If you like, keep talking periodically with your companion about what you notice. It will help you keep focused on the effect the food is having on your body.

■ **Slow down.** *If you're like many people, you reach for more food before you've even finished what's in your mouth. Eating more slowly is the first step toward an increased awareness of your relationship with the food you are eating. Pay attention to each bite. Chew it thoroughly and swallow it fully before taking another. It helps to set your fork down after each bite. Eating this way, one mouthful at a time, will allow you to extract the fullest possible flavor from your food and gain the most intense experience from eating.*

By slowing down, you can also begin to pay attention to the impulses, thoughts and emotions that go along with eating. Often these are powerful reflections of other aspects of your life. Are you eating to push away pain or as a way to avoid a stressful situation? Recognizing that you are eating in reaction to emotions or to fill a void other than hunger is the first step toward changing the pattern.

▌Stay calm and focused. *Try to decipher your emotions before starting a meal. Are you relaxed and ready to focus on your food? If so, begin eating. If you are upset about something, you have a couple of options. You can try to resolve the problem before you eat, then let your body relax as you fully enjoy the meal. If that isn't possible, at least acknowledge that you are so concerned about something that it is taking your attention away from your food. Simply being aware that your mind is on a problem will bring you back to the present. Then concentrate once again on eating, knowing you can go back to the problem later. If you absolutely can't take your mind off the problem, wait to eat. If you eat in anger or frustration, you won't enjoy the food and your body won't react to it well, either. For your health and well-being, wait until you can calm down and be more attuned to what you are eating.*

> **"Some eat to live. Others live to eat. It's living while eating that brings the greatest enjoyment."**
>
> David Tate, mindfulness instructor, Miraval Life in Balance

Reality Check

▌

Save the Day

Just as dinner may be your last chance to add healthful food to your diet, the end of the day may be your last chance to do a balance check. If you've been cooped up all day, take a stroll around the block before going to bed. If your day has been frantic, take a few minutes to stretch, listen to music or practice meditation. The same way early mornings are an opportunity to fit in activities that matter most to you, these last moments of the evening can be used to make the day more memorable.

Selected Spas

There are three main types of spas in the United States. **Destination spas** are self-contained retreats where guests stay for a set period of time—traditionally a week—and concentrate entirely on spa activities. **Resort** or **hotel** spas typically offer exercise and treatments, as well as a spa menu or restaurant. Guests at these spas may pursue structured spa programs or use the services of the spa as part of a traditional vacation. Some resort spas, for example, offer packages combining activities such as golf with spa treatments. **Day spas**, located primarily in urban areas, are used on an à la carte basis by the general public.

There are many worthwhile spas in the United States. The following have been selected because they were primary sources of information and inspiration for this book.

The Anara Spa at the Hyatt Regency Kauai
1571 Poipu Rd.
Koloa, Kauai, Hawaii 96756
808/742-1234
Open-air treatment rooms that let in warm tropical breezes and outdoor lava rock showers set the mood at this relaxing seaside resort spa. Shiatsu and Hawaiian lomi-lomi massages are specialties you'll find here, along with Kapu Kai, a sacred `alaea clay and bath treatment found only in Hawaii.

Bonaventure Resort and Spa
250 Racquet Club Rd.
Fort Lauderdale, Florida 33326
954/389-3300
This is an unpretentious, low-key resort spa where guests are well nurtured by the friendly therapists. The scrubs and baths are especially good. There's a full schedule of exercise classes, including aerobics, step, weight-training and water workouts. One of the three restaurants at the resort serves exclusively healthy, low-fat food.

The Broadmoor
PO Box 1439
Colorado Springs, Colorado 80901
800/634-7711
This premier health and sports resort in the Rocky Mountains is famous for its dry and sunny Colorado climate. Golf and tennis were the star attractions until the spa was added in 1994. European-style hydrotherapy is the real focus here, and the full circuit includes Vichy showers, cascading waterfalls, mineral baths, whirlpools and inhalation rooms.

Canyon Ranch
8600 E. Rockcliff Rd.
Tucson, Arizona 85715
520/749-9000
Located in the desert Southwest, this is one of the most renowned destination spas in the country. It's a particular favorite of serious exercisers, with dozens of daily fitness classes and scenic mountain hikes. There are also mountain biking, tennis, swimming and many other sports. A separate life-enhancement program is designed for those who want to lose weight, quit smoking or make other serious lifestyle changes.

Canyon Ranch in the Berkshires
165 Kemble St.
Lenox, Massachusetts 01240
413/637-4100
A younger sibling of the Tucson spa of the same name, this destination spa is in the heart of a major historic and cultural area. Sports are plentiful year-round, with cross-country and downhill skiing emphasized in the winter and hiking, cycling, canoeing and rafting in the warmer months. You'll also find specialized lifestyle counseling and programs at the spa's Health and Healing Center.

The Claremont Resort and Spa
Ashby and Domingo Avenues
Berkeley, California 94623
510/549-8552
This classic resort has a complete health club as well as a wide array of spa treatments. Of particular note are the one-on-one stretching and restorative yoga sessions. Special spa weekend programs held throughout the year present guests with information they can use when they return home on food, fitness and relaxation.

The Cooper Aerobics Center
12230 Preston Rd.
Dallas, Texas 75230
800/444-5192
Founded by Dr. Kenneth Cooper, the "father" of aerobic exercise, the Cooper Aerobics Center includes a research center, a medical center, a large fitness center and a seven-day live-in Wellness Program that concentrates on fitness, nutrition, group recreation and strategies for a healthy lifestyle.

Doral Golf Resort and Spa
4400 NW 87th Ave.
Miami, Florida 33178
305/592-2000
Built in the style of an Italian villa at a golf resort, this spa provides a wide range of beauty and body treatments for vacationers as well as counseling in fitness, nutrition and behavior for those interested in lifestyle change. Gourmet spa cuisine is a highlight. Yoga and t'ai chi classes are especially well done.

The Golden Door
Deer Springs Rd.
PO Box 463077
Escondido, California 92046
619/744-5777
This destination spa near San Diego has been setting spa industry standards for more than thirty years. Founder Deborah Szekely planned it as the embodiment of the mind-body connection, with its serene Japanese-style settings and a blend of fitness classes and body treatments. Much of the food at the spa is grown in organic gardens and orchards. This is a perfect place to be completely cared-for during a week away from home. Occupancy is limited to thirty-nine women (there are also a few men's and couple's weeks offered each year).

The Greenhouse
PO Box 1144
Arlington, Texas 76004
817/640-4000
The luxurious and a touch old-fashioned atmosphere at this destination spa evokes a setting from a Danielle Steele novel. All the guest rooms and action are centered around an enormous swimming pool, where water classes take place all day. Beauty treatments are a big part of the schedule here and include everything from salt scrubs to makeup consultations. Everyone dresses to the hilt for dinner, which includes formal service and elegant table settings.

Green Mountain at Fox Run
Fox Lane, PO Box 164
Ludlow, Vermont 05149
800/448-8106
The purpose of this destination spa is to help people change their relationship with food. Known as an "anti-diet" spa, Green Mountain focuses on altering attitudes and behavior that lead to overeating. The schedule emphasizes exercise as well as classes and lectures with names such as "DePowerizing Food," "Eating Mindfully" and "Becoming a Competent Eater." Losing weight and keeping it off are the goals of most participants, and Green Mountain has a high success rate.

Green Valley Spa and Tennis Resort
1515 West Canyon View Dr.
St. George, Utah 84770
800/237-1068

Hiking is a major draw at this destination spa in the scenic desert lands of southern Utah. The fanciful style of the treatment areas, where each day is assigned a different color, along with the products made of regional ingredients, transform body care here into an unusually sensuous and relaxing experience. In a popular Native American program, spiritual practices have been adapted for spa-goers.

Ihilani Resort & Spa
Ko Olina Resort
92-1001 Olani St.
Kapolei, Oahu, Hawaii 96707-2203
808/679-0079

This resort spa is situated on the 640-acre Ko Olina Resort on Oahu overlooking the Pacific Ocean. This lovely spa, decorated in the colors of the sea, includes airy treatment rooms, a pool, tennis courts and a cafe. It is also one of the few places in the United States to offer thalassotherapy with fresh sea water. Water workouts take place in a saltwater lagoon.

Lake Austin Spa Resort
1705 Quinlan Park Rd.
Austin, Texas 78732
800/847-5637

This outdoor-oriented destination spa is casual and laid-back. Cottages overlook a large lake, and many of the aerobic activities—canoeing, sculling, waterskiing—are water-oriented. There's a real Western flavor to the food and atmosphere. Each week guests are treated to a low-fat Mexican buffet, and line dancing tops the list of activities. Skin and body treatments come with enticing names such as the Blue Lagoon and the Texas Two Step.

Miraval Life in Balance
16500 N. Lago del Oro
Tucson, Arizona 85739
800/825-4000

Opened in 1995, this destination spa is based entirely on the concept of mindfulness, defined here as a way to put life in balance. Spectacular grounds set amidst Tucson's Santa Catalina foothills include three swimming pools, gardens, a riding stable and tennis courts. Among many activities, guests can take advantage of a variety of two- to three-hour workshops that emphasize awareness training and apply mindfulness to eating, exercise and other aspects of a healthy lifestyle.

Norwich Inn & Spa
607 West Thames St.
Norwich, Connecticut
800/275-4772

This Georgian-style country inn on forty tree-shaded acres is a favorite weekend retreat for frazzled New Yorkers. A full array of treatments includes gentle bodywork techniques designed to balance the body's energy flow. In a couples session you can learn how to massage your partner, and vice versa. Accommodations are in the inn or adjacent condominiums.

The Peaks at Telluride
136 Country Club Dr.
Telluride, Colorado 81435
800/789-2220

This ski-oriented resort spa overlooks dramatic 14,000-foot-high mountains. Those looking for action off the slopes will find it in the spa's indoor and outdoor exercise spaces. There's also a large wet area including an indoor-outdoor pool, steams, jacuzzis and showers. Regional clay and wildflowers are used in facials and aromatherapy massages. Weary skiers will enjoy one of the après-ski packages.

PGA National Resort and Spa
400 Avenue of the Champions
Palm Beach Gardens, Florida 33418
407/627-2000

The spa at this golf-oriented resort offers a full array of beauty and body treatments, selected for guests after a one-on-one consultation, and also offers individual nutrition and fitness counseling. Outdoor soaking pools feature mineral salts imported from therapeutic spots around the world, and low-fat ethnic cuisines are featured in the resort's restaurants. Associated with the spa is the Bramham Institute, which trains spa therapists and offers seminars on take-home spa techniques to the public.

Rancho La Puerta
PO Box 2548
Escondido, California 92033
619/744-7222

Started in 1940, Rancho La Puerta is rich with history and character. Located near Tecate in Baja, California, the Mexican-style spa sits at the base of sacred Mt. Kuchumaa in a landscape of colorful flowers and herbs. Vegetarian food is grown in the spa's own organic gardens and orchards. Hiking and yoga are specialties in a schedule packed with fitness options, while plentiful art workshops, spiritual explorations and inspirational lectures address the heart and mind.

Skylonda Fitness Retreat
16350 Skyline Boulevard
Woodside, California 94062
415/851-4500

Opened in 1994, Skylonda offers vigorous hiking in Northern California forests, along with top-notch stretching, yoga, massage, meditation and low-fat cuisine. Guests sleep, eat and do all their indoor activities in a log-style structure that blends beautifully into the environment. Begun as a destination spa with an emphasis on group participation, Skylonda has become a resort where guests pick and choose among various activities.

The Spa at Hotel Crescent Court
400 Crescent Court
Dallas, Texas 75201
214/871-3200

A private health and fitness club for members and guests of the Hotel Crescent Court, the Spa at the Crescent is a resort facility with an ultra-modern fitness room, personal trainers available for private consultations and a full range of beauty treatments. Facialists here are excellent. There is also a mind-body wellness program for those interested in stress management through counseling, yoga and other mind-body techniques.

The Spa at the Houstonian
111 N. Post Oak Lane
Houston, Texas 77024
713/680-0626

Housed in a 1930s Texas mansion, the Spa at the Houstonian is used primarily as a day spa by Houston residents, but it also offers two- to twenty-one-day retreats for those who want a full dose of pampering. Guests have full use of the enormous fitness facility at the nearby Houstonian fitness club, outdoor pools and tennis courts. Facials, manicures and pedicures are among the best you'll find anywhere, and the atmosphere at the spa is unhurried and friendly.

Spa Grande at the Grand Wailea Resort
3850 Wailea Alanui Dr.
Wailea, Maui, Hawaii 96753
808/875-1234

This seaside resort spa has an East-meets-West philosophy, offering an array of European, American and Hawaiian treatments. The underlying theme is water, and the spa's signature feature is its "terme hydro circuit," a sequence of baths and showers which comes before every treatment. Spa Grande is also known for the Hawaiian form of massage known as lomi-lomi and for unique Hawaiian mud treatments.